HEAVENLY HUMOR

HUMOR

for the

Dog Lover's Soul

HEAVENLY HUMOR
for the
Dog Lover's Soul

75 Drool-Filled
DevotionalReadings
from FellowDog Devotees

BARBOUR
PUBLISHING

Member of the
Evangelical Christian
Publishers Association

Printed in the United States of America.

Contents

SECTION 5—TAIL-BETWEEN-THE-LEGS DISGRACE: OBEDIENCE

SECTION 6—LET SLEEPING DOGS LIE: GRACE

SECTION 7—THE BIG DOGS: GOD'S PROTECTION

SECTION 8—MAN'S BEST FRIEND: FRIENDSHIP

SECTION 9—PUPPY DOG EYES: KEEPING FOCUSED ON THE HEAVENLY FATHER

SINK YOUR TEETH DEEP: GOD'S WORD

I care not much for a man's religion
whose dog and cat are not the better for it.
ABRAHAM LINCOLN

Vending Machine or Banquet?

PAULA SWAN

I have not departed from your laws,
for you yourself have taught me.
How sweet are your words to my taste,
sweeter than honey to my mouth!
PSALM 119:102–103 NIV

Jot came into our lives two years ago. As first-time pet owners, my husband and I had many questions about the behavior of this nine-pound, nine-year-old rescued rat terrier. Why did she eat grass? What compelled her to paw her bedding into a heap? How could she bypass every dime-store drawing pencil on my desk and only bury in the garden the expensive imported pastels?

The most puzzling thing of all was her attitude toward food. The vet assured us that dogs often go twenty-four hours or more without eating after being re-homed, but Jot's appetite didn't improve over the first two weeks. We tried mixing the kibble with water, baby food, wet dog food, and chicken broth. We even heated the food in the microwave to bring out its aroma. Jot ate a few bites of each meal and then walked away. The vet told us not to worry. He determined that Jot had a decreased sense of smell as a normal result of aging, which accounted for her loss of interest in food.

A few days after the diagnosis, we returned from a night out to find a line of paper confetti on the floor. We followed the trail from the front entryway to the bedroom where it culminated in a mound of shredded personal documents that had been tipped from their container. Atop the makeshift haystack sat Jot, contentedly licking a discarded Slim Jim wrapper that had been at the very bottom of the pile.

Since then we've had plenty of evidence that Jot's olfactory function is unimpaired. She grumbles at my pant legs when I come home from the local animal shelter where I've been in contact with cats. She's sniffed out the family of raccoons under the garden shed, the oily spot where a friend dropped a hamburger from the grill, and a box of chocolates under the Christmas tree. Jot doesn't lack ability, but she does need a strong motivation to act.

So do I. I know that the Bible is full of nourishment, but it takes some doing to make me eat. I'll study carefully for Sunday school— if I'm teaching it. There's no problem spending an hour probing the scriptures for a certain verse—if I want to use it in a greeting card. I'll certainly memorize a scripture passage—if I know I'll be called upon to recite it. This habit of scriptural snacking has often kept me from being truly full of God's Word.

Psalm 119:103 describes the Word of God as being "sweeter than honey." Paul urged believers to move from spiritual milk to the more strengthening meat of the Word (see Hebrews 5:12–6:1). In Matthew 4:4 Jesus says, "Man does not live on bread alone, but on every word that comes from the mouth of God" (NIV). The Bible is not a vending machine—it is a banquet. It's time to put away the change purse and pull up a chair.

the Buck Stops Here

DONNA K. MALTESE

"Just as the living Father sent me and I live because of the Father,
so the one who feeds on me will live because of me.
This is the bread that came down from heaven.
Your forefathers ate manna and died,
but he who feeds on this bread will live forever."
JOHN 6:57–58 NIV

Several years ago we had a German-shepherd mixed mutt. We'd gotten him as a puppy and named him after the tag on his cage at the pound—Buckingham Stray.

We have a big backyard but no fence, so we put up a running line for Buck who loved being outside. And although he was glad for a home, he took whatever opportunity he could to shoot out the door and roam the fields and yards of our neighborhood. But he always came back—eventually.

One summer our friend Bob came over to stucco the decaying brick facade of our ancient home. Bob didn't know the rules about Buck. So, unbeknownst to me, while Bob was working on the house, he let Buck out—unleashed—every morning, allowing our mutt to roam the neighborhood unescorted.

One day during this time, I walked around the corner to Pino's Pizza. As I stood at the counter, waiting for my order, Mr. Pino looked at me and then said in his thick Italian accent, "Do you like your dog?"

"Excuse me?" I said.

"Do you like your dog?"

Confused, I responded, "Yes. I do like my dog. Why?"

"Well, ifa you like your dog, then keep him away from my place."

"Buck? Why? What's he been doing?"

"Effery morning, he come and take the bread."

"What bread?"

"Effery morning, he come, take the bread the bakery truck drop off. Fresh. My long, fresh Italian bread, warm. He take it and head down the alley."

"How do you know it's *my* dog?"

"I want to find out why my bread missing. So I come very early. I wait. Your dog come. He wait. The bread man come, then leave. And the dog go up to the box, pull out a long, fresh roll, and head down the alley."

Embarrassed, I apologized profusely, then offered to pay for Buck's thievery.

"No. No money. You just keep your dog home. Yes?"

"Yes," I said, thinking, *Apparently, the Buck stops here.*

Afterward, I related the story to a neighbor who said she'd also seen Buck, just once though, a long roll of Italian bread in his jaws, prancing down the alley, tail wagging. What a treat! For Buck, Pino's bread was like manna from heaven.

Unlike Buck, we don't have to steal our manna from heaven,

for Jesus freely gave Himself for us and to us. He is ours for the asking.

Even better, He fills us every day through the Word. When we are starving for nourishment, His manna, His living Word, provides. Take of it freely. Feed on Jesus every morning before your feet hit the floor.

Chew, Man, Chew

JANICE HANNA

I will delight myself in thy statutes: I will not forget thy word.
PSALM 119:16 KJV

Some dogs are quirkier than others. A few have some, shall we say, unusual habits. Take Bandit, for instance. Even as a puppy, this bloodhound liked to chew, and not the just the usual things. Sure, he liked the occasional dog bone. And he loved a good tennis shoe. But what really got Bandit excited. . .was fabric. He loved the feel of flannel between his teeth, so no blanket in the house was safe.

After losing a couple of really nice comforters and blankets, Cindy, his owner, finally wised up. She bought a small blanket from her local supercenter, just to appease Bandit. If he was going to chew on fabric, at least it wouldn't be her expensive bedding. She prayed this would keep him preoccupied. . .and also prayed he wouldn't swallow any of the fabric!

Less than two months later, Bandit had chewed over forty baseball-sized holes in what was now affectionately called his "chew-chew blanket." Thankfully, he didn't swallow the missing pieces of fabric. Oh no. Cindy found them in a little pile under her bed, neat as you please.

He hid them away like prizes. Still, there was little left of the original blanket. Cindy finally tossed it and bought another, at which point the story repeated itself. She learned through this experience that keeping Bandit focused on chewing the "right" thing solved the problem.

Are you a "chewer" like Bandit? Do you sometimes find yourself chewing on things you shouldn't? Whether we realize it or not, we all do it! Here are a few examples of ways we "chew" on the wrong things. When someone hurts our feelings and we can't seem to stop replaying his or her words in our mind. . .we're chewing. When we refuse to forgive someone for the hurt he or she caused us, we're chewing. And when we have a hard time letting go of a nasty habit, we're chewing. Anything that overstays its welcome is going to end up becoming a problem, if we're not careful. And God never intended for us to chew on things that might hurt us. Just the opposite, in fact!

If you've got to chew, at least chew on the right things. Start with the Word of God. Sink your teeth into it. Spend time meditating on it. Take the pieces you've chewed on and carefully stack them, much like Bandit did, so you know right where they are when you need them. You will find that the more time you spend chewing on good stuff—love, joy, peace, righteousness, long-suffering, etc.—the less time you will have to replay and relive old injuries. Before long, your painful memories will be just that. . .memories. And they will fade more with each passing day as you feast on the Word.

God truly longs for you to be healed of your past. Today, if you're chewing on a past hurt or sin, let it go. Grab a new blanket. . .the Word of God. Then sink your teeth into it. There, you will find the power to move forward.

the Distorted Mirror

DEE ASPIN

When I was a child, I talked like a child,
I thought like a child, I reasoned like a child.
When I became a man, I put childish ways behind me.
Now we see but a poor reflection as in a mirror;
then we shall see face to face.
1 CORINTHIANS 13:11–12 NIV

Aw. . .look at that cute little face." My neighbor stroked Benji's chin, sticky with burs again from some corner in the backyard. His nose twittered like a chipmunk as I clutched him in an upright position against my shoulder.

"Yes, and he's going to dog training tonight for the first time."

My schnauzer's ears perked as Donna questioned, "How old is he?"

"He's three."

Her eyebrows rose.

"I'm taking him because he hops down the street like a rabbit pulling at the leash. . .and. . .he needs socialization. He has no fear of big dogs—any chance he gets he runs straight up to them.

I am afraid of big dogs *for* him."

Donna laughed.

"My little indomitable has run up to two malamutes, cried for a German shepherd, grunted to get near a pit-bull, but backed away from a Chihuahua. He's so used to looking at Sam, his huge Lab brother, and dominating him, he has no fear of big dogs—just little ones. His mirror is warped."

Dog perception can be as distorted as human perspective.

As a child when I saw a small person bossing a much bigger one, I didn't understand it. Then I grew up and learned it's not the dog in the fight, it's the fight in the dog—unless it's a vicious killer junkyard dog. Then we need to stay clear—but Benji doesn't get it.

When I planned for two dogs, a veterinarian advised, "Since schnauzers are so dominant they need to be matched with a big dog that is *not* dominant—like a Lab or a golden."

Big Sammy is so gracious, Benji sees himself in a distorted mirror every day as he bites Sam's legs and hangs off his ears—and gets away with it. He is used to being rough with a big dog who is gentle and who adjusts his degree of play like a big brother toward his smaller sibling. This distortion could lead to serious consequences.

Benji needs a reality check to stay out of trouble. Not all big dogs are safe and tolerant like Sammy. Mirrors with accurate reflections protect us.

I am setting the stage to help Benji discern the real world of dangerous canines, just as our good God teaches us to recognize unsafe people. He uses a mirror of truth, His Word and His Holy Spirit, to portray what we are blind to see because of past distortions and tainted reflections.

Sometimes Christians think all the people they meet in church are nice and angelic. They need to see the true reflection of churches is similar to the world—they can harbor those who take advantage of others.

Hopefully, we can discern the Bible's truths that would help us make wise decisions and keep us from pain as we look in the mirror God is holding up and apply what He shows us.

Maximilian

DONNA K. MALTESE

Love is patient and kind. . . . It does not demand its own way.
It is not irritable, and it keeps no record of being wronged.
1 CORINTHIANS 13:4–5 NLT

In 1973, our springer spaniel Ginger was at the ripe old age of nine (sixty-three in dog years). Dad, afraid Ginger would have a heart attack if he took her hunting again, asked Mom if it was all right with her if he got a new springer pup. She responded with an adamant, *"No!"*

Yet once my dad had set his sights on something, it was very difficult bringing him to heel. So, when we headed to the Jersey shore for the summer, Dad did indeed buy a springer puppy, which he named Maximilian. He just didn't tell Mom. Instead, he took care of Max during the week while he was practicing law at our Pennsylvania home. When Dad came to New Jersey on the weekends, Grandma took care of the pup.

One summer night, Dad took me and my sisters aside and, in an attempt to enlist support that might later be needed, told us all about the cute little springer waiting for us at home. But we weren't to tell

Mom anything about him. Giggling, we promised to be mum.

Unfortunately, our veterinarian, a family friend, knew nothing about the code of silence. On a visit to the beach, he happened to say to Mom, "Christine, I *love* your new puppy."

Mom's face turned to stone, and her voice became stilted as she responded with "*What* new puppy?"

"The male springer Will brought in for shots. . ." The vet's voice faded as he quickly picked up on the fact that Mom seemingly knew nothing about the new addition to our family.

Once the "dog" was out of the bag, Dad brought him to the shore. Maxi was much more affectionate than Ginger and less attached to Dad, much to our delight. We enjoyed watching Maxi dig for shells, swim in the ocean, and hunt frogs under Ginger's tutelage. And the two seemed to get along well, as long as Maxi kept his snout far away from Ginger's bowl at dinnertime.

The vet's visit was a great family story for years, but recently Mom told us she'd known all along that Dad was determined to get a new hunting dog. She just thought it would be easier on her, as far as having to housebreak a puppy, if she pretended to be ignorant of Dad's subterfuge. (And the irony of it is that Dad's new hunting dog turned out to be gun shy.)

In all aspects of their marriage, Mom lived out the precepts of 1 Corinthians 13:4–5, with her patience and keeping no record of wrongs. A good thing, too, for that same summer, Mom got lots of practice. About a month after spilling the beans about the new puppy, the vet came down a second time and said, "Chris, I *love* your new motorboat."

Mom's response? "*What* new boat?"

A PLACE TO CALL HOME: BELONGING

*My dog does have his failings. . .but unlike me,
he's not afraid of what other people think of him
or anxious about his public image.*

GARY KOWALSKI

true Identity

PAULA SWAN

How great is the love the Father has lavished on us, that we should be called children of God! And that is what we are!
1 JOHN 3:1 NIV

The rescue organization for which my husband and I volunteer as foster parents requires that each animal be microchipped with a unique identification number. When seven-year-old Kloey, a rat terrier, came to live with us, the rescue coordinator sent me the chip, the inserter, and a two-page explanation of the procedure. One look at the size of the insertion needle told me that it was a job for my well-seasoned vet and not for a squeamish foster parent. Kloey was going to the vet the next afternoon, so I took the chip along.

After the initial exam and vaccinations were completed, the vet tech asked if I wanted to watch the microchip procedure. I hesitantly agreed. I tried to make conversation to cover my shakes.

"I've never used the scanner," I said. "How do you do it?"

Dr. B. lifted up what looked like a very large plastic magnifying glass and ran it along Kloey's shoulders as he said, "You just do this—" He was interrupted by a single electronic beep. To our surprise, Kloey already had a chip.

Back home, as I waited on the microchip company's customer service line, a myriad of thoughts drowned out the hold music. What was Kloey's original name? How did she wind up on the city streets so long ago? Most importantly, would she be welcomed back home?

The music stopped abruptly, and a woman with a cheerful voice verified the chip number as one that had been assigned but never registered. My heart sank. A nonregistered chip meant that there was no address or phone number on file for the dog. My questions wouldn't be answered, and there would be no heartwarming family reunion. What a difference some identification could have made.

As our world becomes more and more populous, identity becomes ever more relevant. No one wants to say, "I'm just one of four billion. I'm nobody. Don't notice me." We spend a great deal of money and effort protecting our identities from theft. We safeguard our computers, our bank accounts, and our credit cards.

When it comes to our spiritual identity, we can relax. It is ensured by God Himself. In Isaiah 49:16, God says, "I have engraved you on the palms of my hands" (NIV). God promises that even foreigners who choose to please Him will be given an "everlasting name that will not be cut off" (Isaiah 56:5 NIV). How much greater is the promise to those He calls His own? The New Testament states that all believers are "God's children" (Romans 8:16 NIV). We are also a "royal priesthood, a holy nation, a people belonging to God" (1 Peter 2:9 NIV). Our names are even recorded for eternity in the "Lamb's book of life" (Revelation 21:27 NIV).

Kloey's chip is now registered in the name of the rescue group. No matter where she goes, she will always have an identity, a name, and a place to call home. As do we. Praise God for our identity in Christ.

tender traces

DEE ASPIN

"I will not forget you! See, I have engraved you on the palms of my hands."
ISAIAH 49:15–16 NIV

This morning I crunched my torso in partial agony while attempting sit-ups at the gym. Hands clasped behind my head, I propelled my nose straight to the edge of my knee. Immediately, my eyes zoomed to a small familiar blade of hair hugging my stretch pants. *Positively Sam.* No one knows a dog hair like the owner.

In a lifetime, we have spent hours carefully targeting, plucking, and examining the real thing from cars, sofas, and clothing. We learn never to wear black or navy, especially if we are going out and the car hasn't been cleaned recently.

"You have hair on your coat," I'll hear while feeling light brushing against my back.

"Oh, it's my dog," I answer, never skipping a beat. People who have critters chuckle. Others may think we never do laundry; or worse, our dogs are not trained and jump all over us.

Sammy never jumps. He wriggles all around, which has the effect of a giant inner tube spraying water. But unlike a water droplet, each hair does not slide—it sticks. But it doesn't bother me as much as it used to. For always, as today at the gym, every hair reminds me of his presence.

There's just no escaping the fact that Sam is my dog. His traces stubbornly follow me. Yesterday, sitting in the church pew, I glanced down at my plaid skirt and discovered a small line unlike the pattern. He leaves samples of his beautiful strawberry-blond coat everywhere he goes, something he can't help and I can't prevent.

If he lived outside the house, perhaps it would be less obvious. I would spend less time vacuuming and removing dog hair and discovering new and better tricks of the trade. (So far duct tape is the best.)

But I could never leave my dog out in the cold. Shedder or non-shedder, my dogs stay with me. And whenever I see traces of their presence, I find myself whispering a quick prayer of protection for Sam and his little brother Benji-bo.

In a way, we are like that to Jesus. He lives with our brand on His body. He carries it around with Him wherever He goes, because He chose to come down here and walk with us. To rub shoulders with those He created, to romp with us and live with us.

And so He remembers us. He speaks our names. He prays for us all the time from heaven whenever He thinks of us—which is often. Psalm 139:17–18 (NIV) says His thoughts of us are more numerous than the grains of sand on the sea: "How precious to me are your thoughts, O God! How vast is the sum of them. Were I to count them, they would outnumber the grains of the sand." He is always aware that we are His forever. He has only to look down at His hands.

Called, Chosen, and Set Apart

JANICE HANNA

For he chose us in him before the creation of the world to be holy and blameless in his sight. In love he predestined us to be adopted as his sons through Jesus Christ, in accordance with his pleasure and will—to the praise of his glorious grace, which he has freely given us in the One he loves.

EPHESIANS 1:4–6 NIV

Max, a six-month-old half-breed pup, had lived at the puppy mill longer than most. The folks who ran the place had over two hundred other purebreds to offer—darling little things with fluffy coats and perky ears—so he was placed in a cage at the very back of the lot with another half-breed. Max knew he was different, but tried not to let it bother him.

People came and went, oohing and aahing over the expensive puppies, snatching them up and taking them to new homes. Max kept a watchful eye out, wondering if anyone would ever want him. In his heart, he doubted it.

Time went by and Max learned to adapt to his environment. He enjoyed the company of the other dog in his cage. And though the owner of the puppy mill didn't pay them much attention, life was relatively easy. He got fed every day at the same time and always had water to drink.

One evening a family appeared to buy a puppy. They didn't know they were coming to a puppy mill. They were simply responding to an advertisement in the paper. . .about Max! He watched as the father, mother, and daughter walked down, down, down the long row of cages, finally stopping at his. Could it be? Were they really here to see. . .him?

When the nice lady reached down and picked him up, Max was so overwhelmed that he cuddled against her neck and didn't move. And he stayed cuddled against her for over an hour as they drove to her home. His heart raced with excitement. Finally! Someone wanted him! He belonged! How wonderful it felt.

Do you sometimes feel like Max? Do you feel "caged up" by your insecurities and imperfections? Are you keenly aware of your flaws while others around you seem to be basking in the glow of perfection? Do you know what it's like to watch others garner attention. . .to receive praises while you observe from a distance, wondering if you're ever going to be picked?

Here's the good news. God picked you! From before the foundation of the world, no less. You are called, chosen, and set apart. God reaches into your "cage" and scoops you into His arms, where He longs for you to cuddle your head against His neck. . .and enjoy the ride home.

Today, allow the Creator of the universe to free you from the cage you've been living in. Hold your head up high, knowing you belong to Him, and sensing His undying love for you as He carries you through life's many challenges.

the Illusion

PAULA SWAN

Now we see but a poor reflection as in a mirror; then we shall see face to face. Now I know in part; then I shall know fully, even as I am fully known. And now these three remain; faith, hope and love.
But the greatest of these is love.
1 CORINTHIANS 13:12–13 NIV

My patent leather shoes were polished to a brilliant shine. My carefully brushed brown linen jacket showed not one single white dog hair and my silk blouse had a faint aroma of cedar chips from my closet. I had kept my skirt wrinkle-free by standing and holding the overhead strap for the entire half-hour bus trip. Even my nylons were perfect—by judicious placement of treats on the floor, I had managed to get out the door without a single paw coming anywhere near them. I had finally made it to my first important interview, and I looked great.

With the enormous confidence brought on by a good hair day, I entered the personnel office. Smiling broadly, I extended my hand in good will. Four little black "doggie clean-up bags" slid out of my slick silk sleeve and floated down onto the carpet, landing with the softest of whispers.

As I stooped to pick up the bags and tried to think of something appropriate to say, the personnel director crouched down beside me and said, "I've got a Samoyed."

The illusion of perfection I'd tried to create had been humorously stripped away in those first few seconds, and I felt myself relax. We spent twenty minutes talking about our dogs, and only ten minutes talking about my résumé. In that brief time we developed a mutual trust, and it has bloomed into a permanent friendship. After five years of working together, she knows me as a dog lover who prefers senior pets, longs for an off-leash park, and rarely, if ever, wears nylons. I know that she reads dog food labels, keeps up with the latest in veterinary medicine, and once accidentally dyed her dog's hair during an Easter egg-coloring session. Clients and visitors to our office see the workplace illusion they expect, but my friend knows there are still plastic baggies up my right sleeve.

It is said that the secret to success is not what you know, but who you know. I propose that the vital factor is *by whom you are known*.

I think the apostle Paul would agree. He was a citizen of the Roman Empire and had the privilege of being educated by the finest of teachers. He was entrusted with enormous power by the religious authorities of the temple. He knew Pharisaical law and kept it as perfectly as anyone could. If anyone had a reason to feel he was on the fast track to success, it was Saul of Tarsus. Then God came near and everything changed. So great was the power, so blinding the light of God's presence, that this giant among men could only ask, "Who are you, Lord?"

Erudition doesn't impress God. He isn't tricked by titles or degrees or social rank or any of the other temporal and illusory shows of strength to which we so often resort when cornered. He sees right through all of that, knows who we truly are, and He loves us anyway. How magnificent it is to be known by God.

PUPPY LOVE:
DEVOTION

The most affectionate creature in the whole world is a wet dog.
AMBROSE BIERCE

Hide and Seek

PAULA SWAN

"The LORD your God is with you, he is mighty to save. He will take great delight in you, he will quiet you with his love, he will rejoice over you with singing."
ZEPHANIAH 3:17 NIV

Long before we adopted our first dog, I had the itinerary of our human-canine relationship perfectly worked out. We would take quiet walks in the park, people in front and the dog heeling expertly on the left. There would be obedience training (in which my dog would surpass all expectations) and, of course, there would be games of fetch. Lots and lots of fetch.

Naiveté does have a certain charm, doesn't it?

Two years and three dogs later, I am no longer deluding myself. Our rat terriers love the park—for running, not walking—and absolutely not quietly. Kloey is an inveterate barker.

Jot went to obedience training. For six weeks she hid under the chair. In the final two weeks she emerged, but only to steal other dogs' treats before scuttling away to eat them in private. On graduation day the trainer was complimenting each owner on the accomplishments of his or her dog. "Good sit," he would say, or "Way to do a down stay!" When he got to me he thought for a moment and then said, "Well. . .she's learned that a German shepherd can't fit under that stool."

Despite a few setbacks, I never gave up. When Tilly joined our family, I got out the old tennis ball. All three dogs watched the ball bounce, roll, ricochet off the table leg, and come to a spinning stop. They yawned, stretched, and lay down for their midmorning nap. I tried again with a mint-condition rope toy, an unchewed squeaky rubber shoe, and a still-pristine ball of yarn. My dogs have perfected the art of ignoring toys.

The only game Tilly *will* play is hide and seek. One morning when we were running late for a vet appointment, I found her on the windowsill behind the draperies. She tucked up her legs to make a compact bundle, but a bit of plumy tail poked out between the blinds and gave her away. She won't willingly endure rain even when she really needs to go out. During one particularly drizzly week, I found her curled around the drainpipe below the kitchen sink. When the sun sets and she knows bedtime is approaching, Tilly will quietly slip between the upholstered flaps of the fold-out couch.

No matter where she hides, I always find Tilly. That wiggly tail gives her away every time. When I drag her out from under the bed or coax her away from the shrubbery or disentangle the blankets to free her from the laundry basket, I always laugh. I can't help myself. . .those big brown eyes. . .those floppy, spotted ears. . .and that tail! She captivates me. She is my delight.

My dogs aren't what I thought they would be, but they are just perfect. Zephaniah 3:17 tells us that God feels the same way about His children. Imagine His happiness as He finds you, gently calls your name, and frees you from a tight spot. He rejoices over you. He sings joyful songs about you. In God's eyes, you are perfect. You are God's delight.

Arrivederci Prosciutto

DEE ASPIN

"You are the God who sees me."
GENESIS 16:13 NIV

Donna is a natural cook—straight from the Italian section of New Jersey. To my delight, she and her Italian husband, Larry, schlepped over to our West Coast neighborhood. They brought their two dogs, Vinnie and Alee. What breed? What else? Italian greyhounds.

Now, Italian greyhounds are a small version of a racehorse. At rest they are couch potatoes, but when active and alert, they are dynamic dog-racing machines.

Today Donna told me about her little sleuth, Vinnie. He is as smooth as my Labrador, Sammy—his big buddy—is clumsy.

One mild fall afternoon after work, Larry and Donna invited a special guest to their new home for a barbeque. They have a beautiful pool and beautifully groomed yard. Everything was in place, including her Italian appetizer. It was beautifully laid out—each piece of expensive prosciutto slipped carefully in a wedge of honeydew melon.

Larry was busy showing his guest around the yard when Donna stepped inside to the kitchen, which overlooked the yard. As she prepared a salad at the sink, she glanced outside. She stopped and stood staring out the window, her mouth agape.

She watched as Vinnie slowly slinked onto the patio chair and pressed his little muzzle into the appetizer—more precisely, the prosciutto. He gently gripped the edge of the specialty ham and slithered it out of the melon, leaving the melon in place—much like we play Jenga and carefully remove each piece so nothing else moves.

It worked. Larry came back and didn't even notice the one naked little melon. Sammy sat by the table in perfect obedience. Eyes wide. No one knew he had silently digested the delicious prosciutto—that is, no one except Donna.

Sometimes we think we are just as coy as Vinnie. We think no one is looking and we have it all figured out. We know just how to get what we want. And we know how to act like we didn't do anything wrong.

For all our denial, God always sees what we are doing. Just like Donna watched from the window, God sees our sneaky ways. He knows our heart even if we have great poker faces.

Vinnie has dog treats, and they are much better for his sensitive digestive tract than processed meats. And we are better off with a few cookies than a dozen at once. We need limits, and we need to be asked the hard questions. It is for our good.

Next time we find ourselves checking to see if anyone is watching, we need to ask, "What is wrong with this picture? Why am I afraid of getting in trouble?"

Maybe what we are doing is not good for us or takes from someone else and that is why we are looking around. As we learn to trust His love and realize He sees everything, rather than following Vinnie's lead, we will acknowledge God's view and reconsider.

toby knows!

MILLIE MCCLOY

Trust in the LORD with all your heart, and lean not on your own understanding; in all your ways acknowledge Him, and He shall direct your paths.

PROVERBS 3:5–6 NKJV

Toby leaped from his rug and raced to the front door even before he heard the keys jingle in the lock. Bryan was finally home. Toby's tail whipped in unison with his body. Toby's infamous wag had been known to fell even the strongest of men.

Bryan entered the house and laid aside his briefcase and newspaper. Toby looked up adoringly as Bryan leaned down to smother Toby with a powerful two-handed hug. Toby could not understand a word Bryan was speaking, but it didn't matter. He often questioned his master's words. But Toby knew by the tone of the words and by the feel of his touch that his master was as happy to be home and see his puppy as Toby was to have him home. Toby was secure in his master's love.

After a lengthy snuggle, Bryan grabbed the paper and headed for the couch. This was the favorite part of Bryan's day. Not Toby's!

Before Bryan could seat himself, Toby had bounded onto the couch and placed himself comfortably in Bryan's spot.

"Hey, buddy," Bryan said, "we'll get there. Be patient."

Toby was always a little anxious to get outside and play.

A short time later, the two of them slipped into the kitchen to scan the refrigerator for clues to supper. Dried up casserole, a wrinkly cucumber, an open can of soda, and lunch meat. The choice was equally as narrow for Toby. Dried doggie doodles or dried doggie doodles. Toby opted for the dried doggie doodles (and they tasted a lot like chicken!). He had eaten the doodles every day, every meal, for as long as he could remember. It simply didn't matter. He was thankful his master cared for him and provided all he needed.

Watching Bryan clear the table, rinse the dishes, and load the dishwasher was almost painful for Toby. This was now playtime. Toby retrieved the leash and dropped it appropriately at Bryan's feet. Bryan laughed out loud. Toby loved the sound of his master's laughter and delighted in spending time with him.

The two of them wasted no time rushing out the door and across the cul-de-sac toward the park. The park had a lengthy walking path winding around and through it. Toby's step didn't skip a beat; Bryan labored to keep up. It was uncertain to any observer who was leading who. The look in Toby's eyes was clearly understood: Toby knew his master would always be beside him. Maybe not literally at this moment, but figuratively.

That night as the pup lay in bed at Bryan's feet, Toby knew deep in his heart that he was loved. Toby knew he would always be safe in the loving care of his master.

God loves us—so much. He wants us to always know His love and rest secure that He will provide all that we need and more. We can trust that God cares for us and longs to spend time with us and, yes, even longs to laugh and be joyful with us. Just as Toby rejoiced when he heard his master, so should we rejoice upon every remembrance of Him.

Long-Eyed Enduring Love

SHELLEY LEE

Love bears up under anything and everything that comes, is ever ready to believe the best of every person, its hopes are fadeless under all circumstances, and it endures everything [without weakening].

1 CORINTHIANS 13:7 AMP

Early one morning I heard Zoey barking wildly in an apparent flurry of activity. By the time I got to the front porch, I found her with a guilty, wide-eyed, pitiful face, next to my overturned, all-but-trashed, previously beautiful big pot of pansies.

It looked like a mouse had burrowed into the dirt and she'd had to protect the place. I could tell she was guilty. Her sheepish walk gave her away when I called her closer. Her quick obedience to "sit," then "lay," then "hush up!" was incriminating!

Her long sad eyes were still filled with love for me as she lay there watching me clean up the mess, replant the flowers, and then forgive her.

A few mornings later the same thing happened, but this time two flowerpots were overturned, and I was not so forgiving. I corrected Zoey harshly, and she walked even more slowly when called.

She curled up in a ball after taking her scolding and looked at me longingly, with love still in her eyes.

One of my sons joked around, talking for Zoey: "You can learn from me, Mom. Just love. Love like I love."

I grinned, thought about that for a second, and dismissed it just as quickly.

A few days after that, there was a third occurrence, this time on the back deck with three pots of flowers.

I was livid with Zoey. Each time she clearly acted and appeared guilty. "Zoey!" I huffed, broom in hand, to clean up another pointless mess. I scolded her and angrily went about my business.

That's when my husband gently pointed out that Zoey hadn't been out all night, nor had she been out prior to him spotting the crime scene.

He was right, and I felt horrible. Moreover, as I recalled each dirt-flying mess, I realized that Zoey never had any dirt on her paws or nose. Still she'd stood there, taking on the guilt, when it could not have been her at all. She probably thought she was being scolded for not catching the criminal. She'd been framed!

By whom, though, was now the question. And I intended to find out. The cat certainly had it in for her, but it was more likely a raccoon or groundhog.

The next night, extra lights were left on and the front door was left open, with only the locked glass door between Zoey and the unknown criminal. This sounded like a setup for a broken door. I thought about that possibility, but really, Zoey's all bark. Turned out, no broken glass and no criminal either.

Next night, same drill, and Zoey slept right through the criminal activity.

By the time I remembered that human hair keeps away plant and flower eaters, my pansies were reflecting the gray face of death. I, however, had learned a life lesson.

The ability of a dog to love its family is always astounding. It is a great picture of how God loves me. He watches me in my fits of anger, often based on misunderstanding, and loves me still. He took on all my guilt and shame at the cross and He always responds to me, no matter what, with longing eyes filled with love.

Belly Up

JANICE HANNA

*I will lie down and sleep in peace, for you alone,
O LORD, make me dwell in safety.*
PSALM 4:8 NIV

Ginger was a black Lab with a lot of personality. And talk about loyal! She would do anything for her master. When he told her to sit, she sat. When he told her to roll over, she rolled over. When he tossed the ball, she fetched it. Anything he would ask her to do, she would do. Why? Because she sensed his love.

Ginger's favorite days were the ones they spent together, just the two of them. She would curl up at her master's feet or even lay her head in his lap, comfortable and content. Oh, how loved she felt. How safe.

One of Ginger's favorite pastimes was to let her master rub her tummy. She would roll over onto her back and wriggle until he noticed her. He always smiled and spoke words of love over her as this transpired. Then, as he reached down to run his hands along her belly, she would lie perfectly still, enjoying his touch. Before long, she got so relaxed she would fall asleep under his watchful eye. How wonderful it felt to know she was loved. And how she trusted him!

We have a lot to learn from Ginger, don't we? Sometimes we're so frazzled by life that we forget we have a trustworthy Master. And we're so busy that we don't draw near to spend intimate, quiet time with Him. He longs for us to curl up in His lap so that He can tell us how much He loves us. That's what being in a relationship is all about, after all. And He wants us to rest easy, knowing He's in control, even when life around us is chaotic.

It's interesting to think about Ginger's belly-up posture. Lying there on her back, she is completely vulnerable. Open. She senses no fear. Her body position speaks of faith, doesn't it? She trusts her master implicitly. In the same way, the Bible says that we can come boldly to our Daddy-God, entering into His throne room, knowing we are loved. There's nothing to fear. And He longs for you to open yourself as you have never done before, sharing your deepest longings, joys, and fears. This is what real relationship is all about!

When was the last time you had quality intimate time with your heavenly Father? Has it been awhile since you've put yourself in a vulnerable position? Today, slip away to a quiet place and put your head on His shoulder. Feel His heartbeat. Listen to the soothing sound of His voice as He speaks words of love. The King of kings longs to be in relationship with you, so why wait another minute? Run to Him today.

OPEN DOGGIE DOORS: PURPOSE AND PERSPECTIVE

Yesterday I was a dog. Today I'm a dog.
Tomorrow I'll probably still be a dog. Sigh!
There's so little hope for advancement.

SNOOPY

Open Door Policy

PAULA SWAN

"Ask and it will be given to you; seek and you will find; knock and the door will be opened to you. For everyone who asks receives; he who seeks finds; and to him who knocks, the door will be opened."

MATTHEW 7:7–8 NIV

On the first truly hot day of summer, Kloey escaped. She managed to squeeze past my legs and through the screen door (and I do mean *through* the screen) in pursuit of a wandering Jack Russell terrier from the next block. I grabbed a leash and my house keys and jammed on a pair of sneakers. In those few seconds, the dogs had vanished. Two neighbors were out watering their lawns.

"You looking for them dogs?" asked the older of the two.

"Yes," I said, relieved. "Which way did they go? In perfect synchrony they lifted their right hands and pointed—the older man toward the south, and the younger man toward the west. I split the difference and headed southwest, cutting across a yard knee-deep in dandelions. I called Kloey's name as I went, occasionally throwing in the magic word "Treat!" but with no results.

For a half hour I wandered the neighborhood, going ever more slowly as the heat bore down on me. Every block or two I'd meet a friendly neighbor who pointed the way—generally the way from which I had just come. Eventually I decided to get my car.

I was a block from home when one of my neighbors waved excitedly and pointed toward my house. There was Kloey, lying in the cool grass under the crabapple tree, panting with exertion. She was as happy as I had ever seen her. She stood to greet me with a wide doggie grin and a playful wiggle of her stumpy tail. Then with enviable nonchalance she trotted up the walk, lifted her right paw, and gave the door two solid thwacks. Kloey doesn't speak English, but her communication skills are excellent. I opened the door.

I got a cold drink for myself and tipped a few ice cubes into the dog's water bowl. As Kloey and I both drank deeply, I wondered at the difference in our perspectives. When Kloey went through the door, I envisioned her getting lost, dodging speeding cars, and hiding from dog thieves. Kloey saw an opportunity to run freely, make a new friend, and roll in something incredibly odorous. For Kloey, there is no fear in going through a door.

The great heroes of our faith had their own doors to walk through. Ruth found a door in a barley field; Esther discovered one in the throne room of the king. Joseph's door was located in the bottom of the pit his brothers dug for him.

Was Ruth nervous? Did Esther fear execution? Were there moments when Joseph sank into depression? Probably so. Humans are like that.

What is important is what happened when the doors opened. Ruth stepped through with dignity and quietness and found redemption for herself and her beloved mother-in-law. Esther entered boldly and rescued her people from a wrath they did not deserve. Joseph entered with faith and forgiveness, and eventually saved from starvation not only his family, but an entire country.

Your door is about to open. Are you ready?

Dogged Determination

MariLee Parrish

*"I, even I, have spoken; yes, I have called him.
I will bring him, and he will succeed in his mission."*
Isaiah 48:15 NIV

It was the beginning of summer and Ezra was so excited to move to the country with his family. Being a city dog, Ezra felt like he had the whole world to explore. It was almost too much excitement for him. In the city, Ezra had fun going to the park with his ten-year-old owner, Jake. But now he could go where he wanted—without a leash!

Ezra and Jake explored for days. They investigated every square inch of the five-acre property. Ezra would dig holes and bury treasures while his boy would climb each tree in the hopes of finding a favorite. This continued for about a week when Ezra and Jake discovered a real problem: squirrels! Everywhere! They were a nuisance, too. Jake's mom would plant flowers; the squirrels would dig them up. Jake's dad hung a bird feeder; the squirrels knocked it down. Jake hid some snacks in his secret fort; the squirrels ate them all. Something had to be done.

Ezra listened intently as Jake commissioned him to keep the yard squirrel-free. Ezra decided right then and there that he would not fail. He loved his boy and would do his very best to complete the assigned task. And so began the dog's life mission to chase away the squirrels.

Each morning after breakfast, Ezra could be seen chasing after the furry little creatures at lightning speed. He'd take a nap, eat some lunch, and then sniff out the next bunch of exasperated animals. This routine went on for years until the old dog just couldn't keep up with the squirrels any longer.

Ezra's desire to please his master can be a lesson to us all. Jesus tells us in Luke 10:27 (NIV) that our mission is to "'Love the Lord your God with all your heart and with all your soul and with all your strength and with all your mind'; and, 'Love your neighbor as yourself.'" The calling is simple and the mission is clear: Love God and love others. In doing this, we are carrying out our purpose for life on this earth. Decide now to follow the mission your Master has given you with dogged determination. Are there any squirrels in your yard?

How Much Is that Doggie in the Mirror?

JANICE HANNA

*If we confess our sins, he is faithful and just to forgive us our sins,
and to cleanse us from all unrighteousness.*
1 JOHN 1:9 KJV

Mandy, the toy poodle, was scared of her own shadow. She shivered at things that went bump in the night, dribbled on the floor when an unfamiliar person stopped by for a visit, and hid behind the sofa when her owner, Laura, ran the vacuum. As time went by, she made small attempts to get over her insecurities, but then something would happen and she would cower in the dark once again.

Laura did everything she could to pull the dog out of her shell. She spoke in a calm, loving voice and made a point of introducing the dog to others in a nonthreatening way. However, the little poodle still trembled with fear, even after coaching.

One thing was particularly troubling. Mandy would occasionally catch a glimpse of her reflection in Laura's full-length mirror. Instead of seeing an adorable curly-haired poodle, the frightened pup got spooked. She ran yelping under the bed, terrified. Sometimes Mandy would emerge moments later, ready to try again. She would ease her way toward the mirror once more. As soon as she saw her reflection, however, she would flee in fear. Mandy clearly didn't like the image in the glass.

Maybe you can relate to Mandy. When you look at yourself, what do you see? Does the image scare you? Do you view yourself the way God views you, or do you run trembling the other way, afraid of your own reflection? If so, it's time to check in with the ultimate image consultant to get His take on things.

Some people spend many years living the Christian life, but never really see themselves as the Lord sees them. What the Lord sees as beautiful, they see as scarred and ugly. What the Lord sees as perfect, they see riddled with flaws. Some continue to beat themselves up for things they did before they came to know the Lord. Others feel insecure over how they look. Still others wonder if they will ever be lovable. These folks find a million reasons to argue with the mirror.

Can you relate? Do you have trouble with your image? If so, the Lord wants to see you delivered and set free.

What is it going to take to get you out from under the bed? When are you going to start believing that you really are who—and what—God says you are? It's going to take some serious time in the Bible. There, you will get a clear picture of how the Lord views you. You also need to spend some serious one-on-one time with Him. When you're in His presence, the Lord will whisper words of reassurance. In that place, you will learn that you are loved, cherished, and valuable. He will also convince you that the past is in the past. Your sins are forgiven and forgotten. In that intimate place, you will learn that who you are on the inside is far more important than who you are on the outside. Best of all, you will get the Lord's perspective. He's the best image consultant ever!

Charge!

DONNA K. MALTESE

Don't jump to conclusions—
there may be a perfectly good explanation.
PROVERBS 25:8 MSG

My neighbor, a Bucks County artist named Louisa Wismer, lives around the corner, about two doors down from the old Wismer factory. Years ago, she and her husband Dick were raising their grandson Ajax. For his sixth birthday, they bought him his very own dog. Trying to teach him a lesson in responsibility, Louisa told Ajax, "You now have something that you have to take care of. It will be up to you to feed him, walk him, give him water, and train him. He is now your charge."

"What's a *charge*?" asked Ajax.

"Well," explained Louisa, "it's something or someone you have to take care of."

The boy stood there, thinking about it. Then he said, "Grandma?"

"Yes?"

"Can I name him? Can I name him anything I want?"

"Sure. Like I said, he's yours, to have and to hold."

"Well, then, I'm going to call him Charge," said Ajax as he patted the puppy's head then gave him a big hug. The pup, a black Lab mix with a white spot on his chest, wagged his tail and licked Ajax's face.

One afternoon a few years later, Ajax was letting Charge run free through the field behind their house. On their way back home, Charge spotted a workman rolling a distance measuring wheel in a nearby parking lot. Not under the restriction of a leash, a barking Charge sprinted over to investigate the stranger.

Alerted by an incessant yet deep *woof*, the workman looked up to see a big black dog heading right for him. In a panic, he looked around to find the probable owner and quickly spotted Ajax. By this time, Charge was right in front of the workman, jumping up and down and barking. In fear for his safety, the man began yelling at Ajax. "Get this dog away from me!"

Ajax, attempting to bring the dog to heel, kept yelling, "Charge! Charge!"

The workman's eyes widened further as he assumed Ajax was commanding the dog to attack. He began yelling louder, "Call him off! Call him off me!"

Louisa, hearing the commotion, came on the scene, and quickly realized what was happening. Soon she had the situation in hand.

As Ajax later led the dog away, the now calm workman said to Louisa, "I don't know why that kid was yelling at the dog to charge me."

Louisa smiled. "He wasn't. He was calling his dog. His name is Charge."

Often we jump to conclusions based on what we've seen or

heard. But if we ask for clarification and are patient when unsure what to think, God will make things clear. All we need to do is rein in our emotions, ask God for understanding, and let Him shine His light on the situation.

It's a Mystery

DONNA K. MALTESE

*God has now revealed to us his mysterious plan regarding Christ,
a plan to fulfill his own good pleasure. And this is the plan: At the right
time he will bring everything together under the authority of Christ—
everything in heaven and on earth.*

EPHESIANS 1:9–10 NLT

One winter afternoon, when our dog Durham, a shar-pei and yellow Lab mix, was less than one year old, I stuck a dark-coated pan filled with sausage into the oven while making dinner. A few minutes later I noticed the faint scent of hot rubber.

Hmm, that's odd. I considered whether or not the dark-coated pan was the culprit, but that didn't make sense since I'd used the pan numerous times before and had had no problem with an odd smell. So, with a dinnertime deadline looming, I ignored the strange odor.

After preparing a dish of macaroni and cheese, I grabbed a potholder to make room in the oven for the casserole. As soon as I opened the oven door, the intense smell of now-*burning* rubber rushed up from the depths of the fiery furnace and assaulted my olfactory. I staggered back, caught a breath of fresh air, held it in, quickly headed back to the oven, and removed the sausage pan.

Then I stuck my head into the oven to see what could possibly be the source of that intense odor. And there it was: Durham's multicolored SuperBall, resting quietly on the top rack in the back. "What? How did *that* get in there?"

Not knowing what to expect from a hot SuperBall, I grabbed a few paper towels and positioned myself for ball extraction. Slowly, I began sliding out the rack, careful not to let the ball roll down and disappear through a hole in the oven floor. Finally, when the ball was within reach, I snatched it up in the paper towels, ran outside, and threw it out onto the porch, where it made a terrific bounce before heading onto the lawn.

After returning the sausage to the top rack, I added the casserole dish of mac and cheese, and shut the oven door. As I continued making dinner, Durham kept bringing me his tennis ball, dropping it at my feet. But I had no time to play. Then he saw the "other dog" reflected in the oven door and growled menacingly at him for a while. I musingly wondered if perhaps the "other dog" had left the SuperBall in the oven.

Life is full of mysteries. Sometimes we solve them. Sometimes we don't. But of this one thing we can be certain: God knows everything and has it all under control. Because He's got a plan, we need not know all the answers to life's questions. God's "on the ball," and He's working it out. So let's rest easy in His arms, being reassured by His Word and His presence.

Pet Control Patrol and People vs. Pets

Shelley Lee

*God spoke: "Let us make human beings in our image,
make them reflecting our nature so they can be responsible for the fish in
the sea, the birds in the air, the cattle, and, yes, Earth itself, and every
animal that moves on the face of Earth."*
Genesis 1:26 msg

It was vet day for our fifty-pounds-of-muscle, wildlife-killing farm dog, Jesse, so we were heading into the city to the animal clinic. It goes without saying that she wasn't city savvy (even though I just said it).

With four young sons and a salivating Jesse who wanted out the driver's side window, it was a seriously long twenty-five-minute drive. At the vet, we survived the waiting room (minimal damage), and we finally succeeded at getting Jesse to stand still on the scale for the second it takes for her weight to register, which is the only way I'd have known her weight, by the way. Jesse greeted the kind vet with a pool of drool as he marveled at her muscle mass.

Everything was good, she was healthy, and the shot barely made her flinch. Success. *Check that off the to-do list and get this brood home* was all I could think about.

It would be impossible for me to forget that we were in need of milk and diapers, not small needs in the population I oversaw. So on the way home we would have to make a quick stop at the grocery store.

It was a mild fall day and I cracked all the windows as much as possible. As soon as I shut the van door, Jesse began to bark wildly. I mean *wild* (reference "wildlife-killing farm dog," also, "fifty pounds of muscle"). She was already drawing attention from passersby. I considered leaving my oldest son, Trevor, in the van with her, but seven years is not old enough and just wasn't safe. I knew Jesse was safe and we would just have to make a run for it. When I say run, what I mean is three kids in a cart with Trevor trotting beside me and helping me throw stuff into the already loaded down cart.

We passed through the checkout in under ten minutes and emerged victorious into the parking lot. *Phew. Almost there,* I thought. Only to find the local Pet Control extended van *(seriously, are they herding them in to the vehicle?)* and its female operating officer waiting next to my now drool-laden van.

"Are you the owner of this dog?"

"Yes. . . ," I say, as I unlock the doors, restrain the dog, and try to contain three little boys escaping the cart with diapers and groceries.

"Do you realize your dog could die in this heat?" and on with a lecture full of statistics and scolding.

"But I—"

"Here is your warning." She handed me a slip of paper, lowering the hammer on my irresponsible pet-ownership behavior, notice of which appeared a few days later in the local blotter.

Yes, it is official. I have a rap sheet with the animal control department (I think that's what you call them, but was afraid to ask). But my children were safe and sound, and when we finally got the dog home she smiled at me (you know what I'm talking about) and ran off to chase a rabbit. It's what she does. Caring for my family is what I do. So, I guess at the end of the day I knew I'd done well. I cared for the animal that God put under my control, and I'd cared for those He made in His image, the ones He died for.

Playing It Safe

DEE ASPIN

"Be strong and courageous. Do not be terrified; do not be discouraged, for the LORD your God will be with you wherever you go."
JOSHUA 1:9 NIV

I had a beautiful English springer named Luke. He was a large field dog who was afraid of the water and would not go further out than where he could stand. I needed to teach him to swim so he could hunt birds." Rose, a rescue worker, talked about one of her favorite dogs.

"Luke loved to retrieve. One day I took him down to some special springs in Oregon. The ledge stays shallow for hundreds of yards, then drops—a perfect setup for training him to swim. I tossed the floater, and he ran as far out as he could in the water to retrieve it. We were a happening team, even working in rhythm.

"Finally, it was time. I threw the floater just past the ledge area so his feet couldn't stay on the ground. Now he would have to swim a bit and paddle to get the floater back. Luke fidgeted. He was anxious. He started to whine, then looked at me and then the floater. He couldn't stand it. 'Get it, Luke,' I urged.

"Then that clever dog located the string in the water and grabbed it. He pulled a bit, let go, and pulled again. He was working the rope from his stance at the edge of the ledge. Without resistance, it floated into his jaws. Then he swung around and looked at me—the plastic buoy sitting proudly in his mouth. Luke did it his way. He wasn't going to swim, no matter how hard I pushed."

Aren't we like Luke sometimes? Given an opportunity for growth, we resist. We either work a situation so we don't have to stretch ourselves or we don't try at all. If we do what we've always done—play it safe—we never find out what we are made of.

Rose knew what her dog was born to do and what he could do. We need to trust that God knows what is in us. He knows our drive, our abilities, the gifts and talents He placed in us more than we know.

Sometimes we are ready for something we were made to do—but haven't had the courage to plunge forward. Like Luke, if we do it our way, we never achieve what we were born to do.

Maybe if something seems just out of reach, God has it that way for a reason.

Luke felt victorious because he held the floater; Rose knew he'd failed. Sometimes we think, *I made it. I won.* But if we did it our way, God may be saying, "You are missing out."

We can trust that our Master and Creator knows what we are made of and made for. He knows how to position us strategically for success—if we allow Him to stretch us with just a little more perseverance or a little more courage.

Chance-snatchers!

CHUCK MILLER

See then that you walk circumspectly, not as fools but as wise,
redeeming the time, because the days are evil.
EPHESIANS 5:15–16 NKJV

Dogs are nothing if not opportunists.

Our next-door neighbors were having a Fourth of July party for their family, and their family has a lot of kids. Between our yards there is only a line of well-spaced shrubs. During the afternoon, four or five of the smaller children were sitting in a row of lawn chairs, eating sandwiches, laughing, and giggling at the games of the older children— and of some silly adults. One girl raised her arms up and back in laughter and joy. In her right hand was about a quarter of a sandwich. My wife was talking to the neighbor next door, and I had my collie Symba out in the yard, playing ball with him before I put him on the leash and took him for a walk. Seeing the girl's arm go up with the sandwich, Symba zipped like lightning between the bushes and behind the row of chairs, and in one leaping motion snatched the sandwich from the girl's hand, landed, and ate it—as cleanly as the slickest pickpocket and about fifty times quicker! Then he ran back to restart our game, tail wagging.

I was shocked, embarrassed, and snickering at the same time. My wife screeched "Symba!" and started laughing, then ran to the girl to make sure her hand was okay. But Symba had snatched the sandwich so cleanly that the girl didn't even notice until she pulled her hand down to take a bite. When she looked at her empty hand, her eyes got wide. But the kids around her had seen it; some gasped, some were giggling even louder. One who knew our dog yelled, "Yaaay, Symba!"

How skillful are you at seizing opportunities? Snatching chances? Seeing it and going for it? Not for yourself, as with Symba, but for others and for Jesus?

Jesus and His disciples ran into a funeral procession; family and friends were taking a young man to be buried. Jesus found out that the weeping mother was a widow, and the boy her only son. He immediately said inside Himself, "This won't stand!" He showed God's power and taught God's mercy by immediately raising the son and happily handing him back to his mother.

Parents brought children to Jesus to be blessed; in one moment He illustrated humility, ministry, mercy, and God's kingdom.

Sometimes I'm good at opportunity seizing, and sometimes I'm not. One little opportunity I love to seize is with unexpected responses to common phrases. For example, when someone at work exclaims "Oh, my Lord!" (or something worse), I'll often reply, "Yeah, He's the One you need to talk to." Or, when they declare, "Lord, have mercy!" often I reply, "Yeah, if He doesn't, we're all cooked!"

But my wife is better at it. While I was merely apologizing profusely for the stolen lunch, she immediately asked the little girl what kind of sandwich it was, then went over and made her another.

An opportunity-seizer; a chance-snatcher. "Redeeming the time."

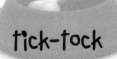

tick-tock

RACHEL QUILLIN

To everything there is a season, and a time to every purpose under the heaven. . . . A time to weep, and a time to laugh; a time to mourn, and a time to dance.

ECCLESIASTES 3:1, 4 KJV

Sara was ecstatic. She'd wanted a puppy from the time she could speak the words. Her parents had been completely opposed to the idea, but when friends of the family offered them a free golden-retriever mix pup, it was too much to resist. They agreed to the offer and Crissy joined the family.

Sara took on all responsibility of Crissy, from feedings and baths to walking and cleaning up after her dog. She even willingly got up in the middle of the night to comfort the scared and whining puppy.

All went smoothly for about a week. Then Sara was invited to her friend's birthday sleepover. "Please," she implored her older sister, Melissa, "can you take care of Crissy just for tonight? I promise I'll make it up to you!"

Melissa wasn't all that crazy about dogs, but she didn't figure one little puppy could be too much trouble for one night, and her mind was already churning with ways she would get Sara to make good on her promise. Of course, she'd never paid much attention to the care Crissy required in the middle of the night. Before Melissa went to bed that night she checked to make sure Crissy had food and water. About half an hour after Melissa fell asleep, she awoke to frantic barking. She waited a couple minutes, hoping the noise would cease. It didn't take too long to realize the puppy wasn't stopping and neighbors would soon be angry. She grabbed a sweatshirt and headed into the night air toward the small shed that had been converted into a doghouse. She sat down on a bale of straw, and the puppy jumped happily into her lap. Melissa couldn't help laughing as Crissy licked her hands and settled in. She stroked the dog's yellow fur, and gradually Crissy settled down. Eventually Crissy crept back to her doghouse. Melissa waited a bit until she was sure Crissy was asleep, then she headed back to the comforts of her own bed.

Melissa had just begun to drift back to sleep when she thought she heard a familiar whimpering. Soon the whimper turned into obnoxious yelps. Melissa sighed and headed out once again. Several times the scene replayed itself. Melissa was nearly in tears herself. On her way out the door the fourth time, she suddenly recalled being told that a ticking clock would calm a barking dog. It sounded weird, but by now Melissa would try anything. She fumbled through her nightstand for her old Mickey Mouse alarm clock, which she placed strategically in the doghouse. Amazingly it worked. Soon Melissa, too, was resting peacefully.

Melissa was reminded there truly is a time and reason for all that happens. In this life we might learn God's reasons for allowing certain events to take place in our lives. On the other hand we might never discover the purpose. The point is to trust God. He sees the big picture. The times of weeping and laughing, the times of joy and mourning are all designed to draw us closer to God and to a deeper relationship with Him.

Something of a Rover

DONNA K. MALTESE

We humans keep brainstorming options and plans,
but GOD's purpose prevails.
PROVERBS 19:21 MSG

Once upon a time in a busy Philadelphia suburb, there lived a dog named Floyd. He was the biggest, sweetest and most handsome, well-tempered springer spaniel for miles around. And because Floyd was registered with the Kennel Club as a champion of his breed, he was a much-sought-after mate for females of his kind.

One day, Floyd's owners, who were also neighbors of my sister Jo, offered her a puppy from a litter they would be having after a quick mating-date in Floyd's backyard. Jo's neighbor was sure the rendezvous would be successful, since Floyd had been through the mating ritual several times before.

The two dogs meet. Floyd feigns interest, plays a little with the prospective mother, then walks away. The female springer is young, attractive, and well mannered but, still, Floyd shows no interest. The awkward encounter lasts about a half hour with Floyd continuing to be unexpectedly stoic and staunchly uncooperative.

Eventually, the frustrated female's owner leaves disappointed, and Floyd's owner is embarrassed and confused. Disgusted with her dog's nonperformance, she leaves Floyd in the backyard hemmed in by a five-foot-high chain link fence.

Sometime later Floyd's owner goes to bring her malfunctioning male inside, but he's no longer in the yard. A search begins. Neighbors help scour the 'hood, but Floyd cannot be found.

About two hours later, Floyd reappears on his front porch. His astonished owner opens the door and Floyd enters, dragging his paws. He gulps down a bowl of water then collapses on the floor, soon falling fast asleep.

Several weeks go by and Floyd's owner gets a call from a friend about four blocks away. There's been an adorable litter of black and white pups. Somehow an unknown male rover had leaped over the four-and-a-half-foot-high cement wall that surrounds her yard and mated with her little dog. And judging from the look of the puppies, the sire was the same male that fathered the female's *last* litter—none other than Floyd!

Floyd's owner, a bit embarrassed, calls Jo and invites her to take a look at the no-longer-mysterious litter. And it was love at first sight for Jo and the puppy she purchased and later named Sadie.

The best-laid plans of dogs and their owners often go awry. When things don't evolve the way we'd painstakingly planned, we may become disappointed, frustrated, embarrassed, or angry. But, as believers, we know that when *God* is involved, His plan will override ours every time—and with His hand in our lives, things will end up working out better than we'd ever imagined! Thank God!

Obedience School Dropout

JANICE HANNA

Blessed is the man who perseveres under trial, because when he has stood the test, he will receive the crown of life that God has promised to those who love him.

JAMES 1:12 NIV

When Beverly adopted a six-month-old cocker spaniel named Princess, she decided to enroll her in obedience school. The feisty pup had several bad habits—chewing up shoes, shredding toilet paper, and barking at the neighbors. Worst of all, she refused to come when summoned. This was especially problematic when Princess wriggled out of her collar on walks. She would take off running across the neighborhood, ignoring Beverly's calls. But surely obedience training would take care of all of that, right?

With great excitement, Beverly showed up at the first class, ready to get to work. The trainer was patient and kind, and encouraged all of the dog owners to be the same. Beverly made up her mind that she would keep working with Princess, no matter how long it took. The first week, they were led through a couple of simple exercises: sit and stay. Unfortunately, Princess ran around the room, completely ignoring her master's commands. The trainer assured Beverly this would get better, if she would just keep working at it. Unfortunately the second week wasn't much better than the first. Princess did manage to sit but refused to stay. And she didn't take to the new commands of "lie" and "speak," either.

By the third week, Princess was the only dog in class who refused to cooperate. Beverly grimaced as the other dog owners showed off the tricks their loveable pooches had conquered. Still, Princess stubbornly disobeyed each command, causing her master great embarrassment. After a while, Beverly began to ask herself, "Why did I even pay for this class? I'm certainly not getting my money's worth." Before long, she and Princess simply dropped out of obedience school. What was the point, anyway?

Sometimes we're like Beverly, aren't we? We set off to accomplish a task that the Lord has given us to do, determined we'll see it through to the end. Our obedience is unquestionable. Then things get hard. . .or don't go as we planned. Before long, we're frustrated, wondering why we ever signed on to do it in the first place. Our determination wavers and our desire to finish well goes right out the window. Eventually, we just give up.

The Bible teaches that we should persevere, to keep on keeping on. God doesn't want us to give up, especially when things get tough. That's the time to dig deep and recommit yourself to a strong finish.

Take a look at the areas of your life where you need to persevere. Have you been tempted to give up? If so, spend some time in prayer today, asking the Lord to show you how you can see that thing through to the very end. Don't drop out of God's obedience school. It's truly the best life training you're ever going to get.

You've Won!

KATHERINE DOUGLAS

*I press on toward the goal to win the prize for which
God has called me heavenward in Christ Jesus.*
PHILIPPIANS 3:14 NIV

And the prizes for the first-place winner include a pair of concert tickets, a dry cleaning gift certificate, a fifty-pound bag of dog food, music CDs, and a gift card for a local restaurant! You can't beat that, folks!"

You sure can't, Judy thought.

"All you have to do," continued the radio host, "is have your dog bark the most times in one minute. I'll count and time each barker on the other end of the phone. You could be the grand prize winner!"

Although the possibility of a win enticed Judy, she didn't own a dog. But Belle, the yipping white fluff ball next door, went ballistic every time she spotted Judy.

Would the radio announcer accept a contestant who didn't own a dog?

The radio DJ laughed when Judy called in and asked if she and Belle could compete in the contest. Somebody who didn't even own a dog wanted to win the barking dog contest? He thought that was hilarious.

Waiting for her turn, Judy stayed on the line, listening to the competition. So far the string of contestants hadn't done well. Percy, Max, and Noodle Poodle barked in varying pitches, but none of them in a rapid staccato. Some contestants whined or howled, but didn't bark. One old dog, not up for any new tricks, only barked twice. None of them had Belle's Gatling gun rapidity.

"You're up next!" Judy heard the announcer say over the telephone.

Judy yelled at her neighbor to let Belle out, and out Belle came, jumping and yipping at Judy right on cue.

Yip! Yip! Yip! Yip! Yip! Yip! Yip! Yip! Yip! Yip! Yip! Breathe.

The counter on the other end of the telephone could barely keep up.

Yip! Yip! Yip! Yip! Yip! Yip! Yip! Yip! Yip! Yip! Yip! Breathe.

Judy laughed until her sides hurt. So did the radio announcer. Belle just kept on yipping.

To be a prizewinner, or have a dog that's a prizewinner, triggers a host of emotions—laughter, happiness, perhaps even pride. Maybe you've never been a prizewinner, and your dog would never win a barking contest. The apostle Paul encourages us to press on for a prize that tops anything we can imagine. When he wrote the scripture above, he sat in a prison cell. No award awaited him before his execution. But Paul didn't have his focus on any worldly prize. From the early days of his ministry, he competed for a heavenly prize. The prize awaiting Paul—the prize that awaits all who set their hope in God—has no equal.

Do you want to be a winner? Do like Paul. "Run in such a way as to get the prize" (1 Corinthians 9:24 NIV).

"You've won!" the announcer told Judy, his stopwatch finger cramped from trying to keep up with the barking Belle.

Judy enjoyed the tickets, gift cards, and music CDs. Belle enjoyed the bag of dog food when she stopped barking long enough to eat.

Max and the Not-So-Mighty Mouse

DONNA K. MALTESE

Unrelenting disappointment leaves you heartsick,
but a sudden good break can turn life around.
PROVERBS 13:12 MSG

My family had a springer spaniel named Max. When he was old, somewhat deaf, and a bit gray around his curly ears, I agreed to babysit him while my widowed mother went away on vacation. At the time, my husband, daughter Jen, and I lived in a small ranch with a black and white cat named Doc, but there was always room for one more.

Max quickly settled into our routine and seemed to get along well with Doc, who merely ignored him, as she usually did the rest of us. And although Max was deaf, I was familiar with the tricks to get him to respond. In order to get his attention, I clapped my hands. He'd then look in my direction. Then I used "sign language" to let him know what I wanted him to do. Waving my hand in a circle toward my body meant "come." A pointed finger meant "sit." And so on.

One day during Max's visit, I was sick with the flu and spent the day lying on the couch, reading or watching TV. During a fit of sneezing, I knocked my tissues off the coffee table. As I retrieved the errant box, pulling it out from underneath the couch, I spotted— horror of horrors—a mouse. Deathly afraid of varmints, my heart began beating furiously. My fifty-pound head rang. I broke into a cold sweat.

I looked across the living room and saw Doc sitting there, licking her paws.

"*Pssssst!* Doc!" I said in a loud whisper.

The cat looked up at me, the epitome of boredom on her whiskered face.

"Doc!" I pointed in the direction of the mouse. "Get it! Get the mouse!"

She looked at the mouse. Looked back up at me, then yawned.

"Doc! C'mon! Get the mouse!"

She looked at the mouse again. Looked back up at me. And left the room.

Tears of frustration coursed down my cheeks. "Stupid cat! What good are you?"

What was I going to do? I would be trapped until my husband came home and rescued me. Panicked, I remembered Max. There he was. Sleeping on the kitchen floor. Ah! Sweet hope!

I clapped my hands.

Max immediately perked up.

I waved my hand. *Come.*

Slowly, Max hoisted himself up off the kitchen floor, then stopped under the archway leading into the living room.

Silently, I pointed to the mouse beneath the couch. Spying the rodent, Max's ears perked, and he rushed into the room, grabbed the mouse between his teeth, chomped, then let the rodent's body drop to the floor. My hero!

Sometimes the people (or animals) we usually count on fail us miserably and our hopes are dashed. Yet others may surprise us in the most desperate of times, making our hearts sing with unexpected joy. The important thing is to not let disappointment rule our lives. Hang on to hope! You never know what might happen or who might intervene to turn your life around.

Please Re-Leash Me

DONNA K. MALTESE

"How can you say to your brother, 'Brother, let me take the speck out of your eye,' when you yourself fail to see the plank in your own eye? You hypocrite, first take the plank out of your eye, and then you will see clearly to remove the speck from your brother's eye."
LUKE 6:42–43 NIV

Our mutt Durham, a yellow-Lab–shar-pei mix, loves to take us for walks. My husband has no problem with this ninety-pound muscled mongrel pulling him down the street. But I need to use the head-halter leash to prevent Durham from wrenching my shoulder from its socket.

This past Christmas I got an MP3 player, which my son helped me load with songs. So the next nice day, I clipped my MP3 player to my coat pocket, looped Durham's leash around my wrist, and we headed out the door. Our first stop was the bank. I walked up to the drive-thru to cash a check. Durham sat there, staring at the pneumatic tube contraption, knowing that on its return, it would bring a dog biscuit with it. We patiently waited as cars lined up behind us. And eventually, the canister came down the tube, containing cash and a doggie treat. Next stop, the post office where I picked up my mail and the postmaster gave Durham another treat. So far, a really productive day.

Next we headed past the tractor store and up the hill so that we could walk to the turkey farm market, then head back home. As we walked up the hill, I retrieved my MP3 player from my coat pocket and began flipping through the music selection. While doing so, I happened to look down at my wrist. My heart stopped in my throat as I noticed that the leash was no longer connected to my arm. In terror, I looked up the road. No Durham. I looked to my right, across the street toward the cows in the field, then at the turkey farm parking lot. No Durham. I turned to the development at my left. No Durham.

Frantic, I turned around and looked down the hill at the sidewalk I'd just traveled, and there he was, about twenty feet away. Sitting. The leash on the sidewalk next to him. And Durham staring at me, with a stupid look on his face.

Immensely relieved, I said, "Good boy, good boy," as I walked over to him, picked up his leash, and we began walking again. "Thank You, God. Oh, God, thank You."

Later that night, I was telling my husband the story, ending with, "And there sat Durham with this really *stupid* look on his face."

Pete interrupted me. "Stupid! Stupid! *He* was stupid?"

And then it hit me. Like a brick. *I* had been the nonsensical one. Not the dog. I was the one who did something stupid and put my canine companion in jeopardy. How could I have been so blind, so hypocritical?

Funny, how we look at situations and see others at fault instead of ourselves. Just goes to show you that Jesus was right. Isn't He always?

TAIL~BETWEEN~THE~LEGS DISGRACE: OBEDIENCE

*Sin is like dog poo; when you get some on your shoe,
a little is as bad as a lot.*

CHUCK MILLER

Oil and Lube Job

JANICE HANNA

No temptation has seized you except what is common to man.
And God is faithful; he will not let you be tempted beyond what you can
bear. But when you are tempted, he will also provide
a way out so that you can stand up under it.

1 CORINTHIANS 10:13 NIV

By all accounts, Copper was a well-behaved miniature dachshund. The loveable pooch spent most of his days lounging around the house, occasionally venturing out to the yard to play. However, you know the old saying, "When the cat's away, the mice will play." One day Copper's owner, Katie, left him alone in the house for a couple of hours while she went shopping. He decided a little investigation was in order and quickly discovered a jar of Vaseline on her bedside table. It didn't take much effort to get that jar down and pry the top off. The contents inside were slippery, but tasty, at least the first few licks. After consuming about half of the jar he gave up, deciding he'd had enough.

By the time his owner arrived home, Copper was feeling a little queasy. More than a little, actually. Katie searched high and low for her pup, but couldn't find him. Copper—one sick little guy—was hiding under the bed. She eventually found him there, along with the half-eaten jar of Vaseline. It took a little prying, but Katie managed to coax Copper out into the open. He came with tail tucked in and head hanging low, knowing he would be scolded. Thankfully, this was one of those cases where Katie felt he'd learned a tough enough lesson already. So had she. The jar of Vaseline went back in the bathroom where it belonged.

After a bit of research on the World Wide Web, Katie realized this situation would probably resolve itself without a trip to the vet's office. Oh, but what a terrible night Copper had. That self-inflicted oil and lube job did quite a number on his tummy. Copper paid a heavy price for succumbing to temptation.

We're a lot like Copper when it comes to sin, aren't we? We see something just beyond our reach, and it's oh, so tempting! With a little extra effort, we manage to snag it and take our first bite, convinced it's going to be wonderful. Eventually, however, reality hits. We realize that we've risked everything for something that can actually bring us harm.

Shame overwhelms us at this point and we hide away in the shadows of darkness, hoping no one will find us. And when our owner—the Lord—coaxes us into His presence, we come with head hanging low. But He welcomes us anyway, convinced we have learned the appropriate lesson from our actions.

In the end, sin is never pretty. In some cases, the consequences are downright ugly. But we serve a God who sees beyond our sin and offers grace and forgiveness when we ask. All He asks is that we come out from under the bed and own up to what we've done.

Copper eventually recovered from his Vaseline encounter. But he stands as a testament to the fact that temptations—no matter how tasty—are better off left on the shelf.

He Lies Like a Rug

KATHERINE DOUGLAS

Keep falsehood and lies far from me.
PROVERBS 30:8 NIV

No one would ever believe a dog could be a liar. There's one dog out there, however, who is. Roebuck has been lying to his canine brother, Sears, for years. Sears' and Roebuck's owners have caught on to Roebuck's duplicity, but not Sears.

These two big dogs, a mix of Irish wolfhound and German shepherd, tip the scales at over a hundred pounds each. Sears favors the German shepherd side of their shared gene pool. Roebuck looks more like their Irish wolfhound heritage. When Roebuck's hair is cut short, his owner says he looks just like G. Gordon Liddy—but that's incidental to the story here.

Roebuck's pattern of lying never changes. Gullible Sears has yet to figure out the awful truth about his brother. As a result, Sears gets hoodwinked night after night.

When the shadows begin to lengthen, both dogs know it's bedtime. Sears wastes no time grabbing the best sleeping spot in the house. Once he plops his bulky frame smack-dab in the middle of the bed, he emits a long, contented sigh and settles in for the night.

After the prime sleeping spot is warmed and ready, Roebuck wanders into the room nonchalantly. He walks to the window. He looks outside. Suddenly, his entire posture becomes erect. With his focus locked, he plants his feet on the windowsill. Looking out the window, Roebuck begins barking for all he's worth.

Sears' head jerks up, his ears as pointed as two sentinels.

What's out there, bro? What do you see?

Sears can't stand the suspense. He's got to investigate for himself. He jumps up from the sweet spot to join his barking brother at the window. While he looks up and down the street, he primes his guttural pump. He's ready to let it rip with his own commanding bark.

Quick as a racetrack dog, Roebuck bounds up on the warmed bed. While Sears looks to the left, to the right, and back again, Roebuck's eyes have already closed. By the time Sears comes to the conclusion that there's nothing outside worth looking at—let alone barking for—Roebuck has snuggled in Bed Central. Sears is left to lie down on the fringes of the mattress. He's never figured out that his own flesh and fur lies like a rug.

What lie or lies do we fall victim to? The one that says, "If I had more money, I'd be content"? The infamous "it doesn't hurt to window shop" adage? The "do it your way" maxim? Truth to be told, we've all believed a lie at some time.

We're warned throughout the pages of the Bible that the devil is "a liar and the father of lies" (John 8:44 NIV). Let's not get fooled by the enemy or those who try to lead us astray with deception or lies. Let's not be lured to look out the window like Sears. No matter how convincing the bark that entices.

Pride Goeth

MILLIE McCLOY

Pride goes before destruction, and a haughty spirit before a fall.
Better to be of a humble spirit with the lowly,
than to divide the spoil with the proud.
PROVERBS 16:18–19 NKJV

Claire, an ostentatious blond cocker spaniel, always prided herself not only on her superior appearance, but also on her humanlike mannerisms. She fairly pranced alongside her master when out and about, with her head held high and her nose straight ahead. Claire's master, Joan, certainly contributed to the false sense of pride with such ploys as matching ribbons tied meticulously over each long ear and appropriately colored nails. Ofttimes Claire could be seen sporting a colorful trendy sweater and hat or a festive poncho and matching bandana—whatever the occasion demanded.

Claire had mastered the ability to communicate with Joan through a pattern of well-placed multi-toned barks, whimpers, and nudges. This certainly endeared her to her master and reinforced Claire's self-assurance, even though it hardly needed more encouragement.

During trips to the park along with Joan, Claire simply refused to even acknowledge the presence of any other canines in the area. With head held high and a bouncy strut, Claire managed to be totally oblivious to anything or anyone other than herself.

One fateful day, however, Claire was forced to experience what you and I refer to as a reality bite (pun intended). Rain had been pouring most of the afternoon. When Joan arrived at the dog sitters, Claire was happy to see her but concerned about getting wet on the way to the car. As expected, Joan cradled Claire in her arms under a bright red umbrella, much to the dog's relief.

The roads were heavily puddled, and the rain was relentless. As she drove, Joan struggled to see clearly through the raging wipers. Suddenly the tires hit water, the car hydroplaned and swung around, landing disheveled on the side of the road. All was still for a moment. Joan was now crying and very scared. She tried repeatedly to restart the car's engine to no avail. Realizing the impending danger of the storm, Joan decided it was necessary to get out and run for shelter. Claire could not believe what was happening. All of her whimpering and barking were inconsequential. She was now running in muddy water up to her chest. She fought to keep her ribbons on but soon lost them both to the murky water. There seemed to be no shelter in sight. They walked for a mile. Then, just as Joan was about to give up, they spotted a small farmhouse near the road ahead. As they jumped the fence and approached the house, Claire spotted a doghouse inhabited by the mangiest mongrel she had ever laid eyes on.

The darkness of night and severity of the storm forced them to accept the humble invitation of the farmers. Claire would be required to share bunks with the mangy mongrel. Joan was invited to share a daughter's room. While Joan partook of a lovely fried chicken dinner, Claire shared a bowl of cold, hard Doggie Bites, but somehow was thankful for even that. The provisions of the cold damp doghouse were humbling to Claire. But she sensed a strange new feeling as she warmed herself next to the mongrel. That night Claire thought about the humbleness she had witnessed at the farm and the thoughtful kindness she and her master had been shown. It was a new idea and a warm one.

It is so easy to get caught up in the show of life. We strive to be cool, to be accepted, to be noticed. Many times we do this routinely without thought, making our appearances the most important part of our day. We pride ourselves on the way we look, our dress, the way we perform our job, our car, our career, our home. But of what value is this pride? What do we gain from it? Does it put God first or us first? Does it glorify God, or does it glorify us?

A Dog's Nose

Donna K. Maltese

Let none of you suffer as a murderer, a thief, an evildoer,
or as a busybody in other people's matters.
1 Peter 4:15 NKJV

Sadie is a leaping, bouncing, happy-go-lucky half-springer spaniel mutt, relatively short in dog stature, with a big box-shaped head and a pushed-in, square nose. This brown and white speckled dog's greatest pleasure is to explore the backyard, which is bordered, in part, by stacked cinderblocks with decorative cutouts, almost like latticework. In her backyard, Sadie can chase leaves, squirrels, birds, and the occasional bunny. But at times she proceeds with caution, for early on in life Sadie learned a valuable lesson in exploration.

One day, when Sadie was one year old, her family members noticed she was missing.

So they started searching. Eventually they approached the back door and noticed Sadie was outside, having apparently gotten through a baby gate and making it to the portion of the yard surround by the decorative cement blocks. Her family members saw her peering out the concrete latticework and said, "Oh, look how cute she is." Relieved, they called her to come inside the house but soon realized her head was stuck between one of the cutouts. They immediately began to panic—vocally and otherwise—not only frightening the puppy, but the youngest child, Lizzy, who kept yelling, "Sadie's going to die! Sadie's going to die!"

Fortunately, a fireman who lives across the street heard the commotion and came over to investigate. Taking one look at the situation, he went back home and returned with tools to cut the puppy loose from her predicament. When he finished rescuing the dog, he quietly packed up his gear and headed back home. All in a day's work.

When a now older Lizzy was asked what she'd learned from the event, she immediately said, "Don't stick your nose where it doesn't belong." A lesson that speaks volumes to all of us.

How often do we pry into business that is not ours? How often do we speak when our opinion has not been called for? How often do we find our own noses stuck in a convoluted piece of latticework and need to have it strategically removed?

Yes, there are things that draw our attention. And there are issues that our mouths beg us to comment on. But often there is another voice in our head that tells us to be quiet. To mind our own business. And that voice is often right.

In four places, the Bible tells us to mind our own business (see 1 Thessalonians 4:11; 2 Thessalonians 3:11; and 1 Timothy 5:13), at one point comparing our meddling to murder, thievery, and doing evil (see 1 Peter 4:15)! That's something to think about!

So before we head out into the world to see what is going

on, we would be wise recall Sadie's early lesson and to remember Lizzy's advice: "Don't stick your nose where it doesn't belong." For it stands to reason that wherever we stick our nose, our head and mouth inevitably follow.

In the Lap of Learning

CHUCK MILLER

Train a child in the way he should go,
and when he is old he will not turn from it.
PROVERBS 22:6 NIV

Puppies love laps.

Right after we brought Symba, our collie puppy, into our home, we had to make three trips between our house in Toledo, Ohio, and Johnson City, Tennessee. It's about an eleven-hour drive, and my wife couldn't stand the thought of keeping the new puppy anywhere but on her lap. We were afraid we might be spoiling him for future car trips, but that's the way he wanted to travel. So off we went, me driving and Rob with little Symba on her lap.

Three trips, to and from Johnson City, with a growing puppy on our laps. It was precious, and he traveled well, but we still thought it might turn out to be a mistake.

It was six months or more after all of this before we had occasion to take him in the car again. My wife opened the back door, meaning for me to help Symba get in the backseat. Then she got in the front passenger seat and—*wham!*—up jumped Symba who landed on her lap, ready to go!

Only this time his front paws were on the driver's seat and his back legs were hanging out the car door! He had a look on his face that said, "Hey, gang, this is cool! Let's go!" After Rob and I stopped laughing ourselves silly and Symba's expression had changed to, "Yo, what's the problem here?" we gently eased him back out the door, and encouraged him into the backseat, which puzzled him.

But only for a moment. After trying to crawl forward between the front seats and onto Rob's lap one last time, he kindly agreed to take up his new space on the backseat. He has been a perfect traveling dog ever since: quiet, sleepy, happy to be with his family. He doesn't even get yappy when he sees people or other dogs outside that he wants to meet. He's as contented back there as when he was in our laps on those trips to and from Tennessee.

An old adage that reflects scripture says, "As the twig is bent, so grows the tree." Although we thought we might be spoiling Symba, that it might be difficult to retrain him to travel without being on our laps, he was, in fact, learning that traveling in a car is a time of peace, a refuge of sorts. He has us within paw's reach, and we, being belted into our car seats, are a captive audience. Our presence makes the car a refuge to him, as God is to us. And that's peace to him, as it is to us. "Let the righteous rejoice in the LORD and take refuge in him" (Psalm 64:10 NIV).

We had trained Symba, without even knowing it, to be at peace in a car. And he has been, ever since.

Double Standard

KATHERINE DOUGLAS

*"Don't pick on people, jump on their failures, criticize their faults—
unless, of course, you want the same treatment. That critical spirit has
a way of boomeranging. It's easy to see a smudge on your neighbor's face
and be oblivious to the ugly sneer on your own."*
MATTHEW 7:1–3 MSG

Amy's dog, Cooper, loves to wander about the neighborhood. Not all the neighbors appreciate Cooper's wanderlust. So to keep the big dog in his own yard—and still give him some freedom—Amy had an electric fence installed. Cooper's electrified collar serves the duo well. Amy knows Cooper will stay where he belongs. Cooper knows a price is to be paid for breaking the rules and going through the invisible fence: an unpleasant *zap*! The arrangement works for both of them and all the neighbors—most of the time.

One day the collar couldn't keep Cooper corralled. Cooper saw something too inviting to ignore. He decided a little pain was worth the gain. Gritting his teeth, Cooper bolted through the invisible fence. The zap didn't slow him down; he was off and running!

When Amy saw that Cooper had fled the premises, she had to go hunt down her dog. She finally found him and led him back home. Cooper came home alongside Amy, his tail between his legs. When they reached their house, Cooper sat his doggie derriere down and wouldn't budge.

No way was he going to get zapped twice! Getting out was one thing—getting back in was something else again. It wasn't worth it. He whined and resisted, easily outweighing Amy. Cooper well remembered his departing jolt. He wasn't about to get another to get back in. Amy finally realized why Cooper wouldn't move.

"Oh! Sorry about that, buddy." She removed his collar, and Cooper immediately went into the yard. Unfortunately for Amy, she followed Cooper into their yard, forgetting what she held in her hand.

Zzzzzzzzzzzzap!

Amy looked at Cooper. Was that the slightest suggestion of a smirk she saw on his muzzle?

How often do we wish secretly for other people to "get what's coming to them"? Whether it's a rude driver cutting us off in traffic, or a coworker whose sloppy work makes our job tougher, we're quick to wish for old-fashioned comeuppance to come down on their heads. From the Old Testament through the New, we're warned about wanting others to get what they deserve—but not us.

King David quickly passed judgment on the rich man in Nathan the prophet's story. "He must pay for that lamb four times over" (2 Samuel 12:6 NIV), David said. What he didn't realize initially was that he was the rich man of the story. He did pay for his sin four times over, just as he himself declared. (See 2 Samuel 12:7–19, 13:23–34, and 16:22.)

In the New Testament, our warning rings loud and clear. "With the measure you use, it will be measured to you—and even more" (Mark 4:24 NIV). Before we point a finger at someone else, we need to consider the remaining three that point back at us. God makes the rules and the judgment calls. Just like Cooper's collar, His rules work the same for all of us.

Ginger's telltale trail

DONNA K. MALTESE

The sins of some men are obvious, reaching the place of judgment ahead of them; the sins of others trail behind them. In the same way, good deeds are obvious, and even those that are not cannot be hidden.

1 TIMOTHY 5:24–25 NIV

My sisters and I grew up with an English springer spaniel named Ginger. My father bought her in Morgantown, Pennsylvania, on an Easter Sunday road trip to my grandmother's house in Lancaster. We three little girls were thrilled to have a brand-new puppy, especially this cute little runt of the litter. But let's face it. From the moment Ginger threw up on our Easter Sunday coats, her heart belonged to Daddy.

Don't get me wrong. Ginger loved spending time with us kids. But Dad was the one who took her hunting, where she was allowed to flush out pheasants and bunnies and retrieve ducks from the water. And once Dad took her off her leash, she never ran away—well, except for that one time when she was wet and backed into an electric fence, but that's another story.

Yes, Ginger loved swimming in the creek by the bungalow and

searching for water snakes in the rocks that lined the banks. When she found a snake, she'd grab it in her jaws and shake her head until the serpent was dead. She stood on docks and barked at geese until they retaliated and bit her on the nose. When we started spending our summers at the Jersey shore, she'd hit the waves as she trailed after Dad. In the empty lot behind our beach house, she'd chase and kill frogs and then spend the rest of the day dripping drool onto my mom's wood floors.

Besides hunting, swimming, and following my dad around, Ginger had an inordinate fondness for trash. Other people's trash. One morning when I was in eighth grade and getting ready for school, my mother yelled up the stairs. "Donna! Ginger's been in the Millers' trash again. Please go over and clean it up before your bus comes."

"How do you know it was Ginger?" I shouted back down.

"Because she left a trail."

I looked out my bedroom window, and there it was. A path of coffee grinds, tin foil, used napkins, banana peels, etc., leading from the Millers' side door, through their yard, across our driveway, and half a foot up our bank. Lovely. And where was the canine culprit? Cowering under my parents' bed.

Like Ginger, although we may, at times, think we're getting away with something, our misdeeds do leave a trail behind us. Perhaps not as obvious as coffee grinds, banana peels, or grapefruit rinds, but they are still there. And although they may not be found out right away, they cannot be hidden forever—from neither people nor God. And it works the same with our good deeds. Some are more obvious than others, but all are eventually revealed.

So today, ask yourself this question: What kind of trail am I leaving behind?

I Prefer a Size 8

MILLIE MCCLOY

Apply your heart to instruction, and your ears to words of knowledge.
PROVERBS 23:12 NKJV

Willie was the cutest puggle in the neighborhood. He lived in an apartment in the suburbs with his owner, Todd. Todd was a graphic artist and was gone for long periods of time during the day. Todd had recently met Willie at the Denver Dumb Friends Rescue Mission. It was love at first sight for both of them. Willie put on quite a show for Todd, hoping, of course, to impress with nuzzling and whining. The decision was an easy one for Todd when Willie placed his right front paw on Todd's hand as he knelt before him.

Through the first few weeks, the two of them grew more and more secure in each other's love and trust, so Willie was adapting to spending time alone waiting for his owner to come home at night.

Todd was teaching Willie to fetch, sit, roll over, and speak. Willie didn't mind performing as long as it meant a walk in the park or a doggie treat afterward. He was quite the showman when necessary.

There was one little problem, however, that Todd was not able to resolve with any training or bribery. Willie loved shoes. Not to wear.

He loved to eat them. He loved them for breakfast, for lunch, for a snack, and any other time he felt hungry. He even loved to eat them when he didn't feel hungry.

Willie was especially fond of tennis shoes, as the soles were remarkably chewy and comforting. But if the occasion warranted, he could be found munching on a pair of sandals or even Todd's dressier wing tips. Willie's appetite was easy to satiate.

As one can imagine, this was not something Todd was willing to accept. Todd had replaced multiple pairs of shoes, and his patience was wearing thin with Willie's behavior. He knew he had to put his foot down!

Early one Saturday morning Todd awakened, made coffee, and dressed for a morning jog. Willie already recognized Todd's weekend routine and readied himself by grabbing the leash and running to the front door.

Willie ran adjacent to Todd, carefree and footloose, enjoying the cool morning air. It wasn't until they reached the fork in the path that Willie became aware of a change in their route. Todd led them to the right and continued down the path on the way downtown.

Shortly they reached the doorway of the north Denver Goodwill store. Todd opened the door and led Willie through the store toward the shoe department. There they found hundreds of pairs of used shoes. All rather odiferous, ragged, and homey. Todd escorted Willie slowly through each row, shoe after shoe after shoe.

Willie sniffed and snuffled and sniffed and snuffled until Todd was sure he wanted to get out of that store! Still Todd continued to lead Willie among the shoes, not intending to miss even one pair. Willie winced and whined, and finally, they started for the door. Todd smiled as he walked outside, then knelt beside Willie. Willie had learned a lesson about greed and obedience that day. Todd had done this solely for Willie's own good. From that day forth, the relationship of dog and owner was firmly footed.

Scents. . .and Sensibilities

JANICE HANNA

Come near to God and he will come near to you. Wash your hands,
you sinners, and purify your hearts, you double-minded.
JAMES 4:8 NIV

Spunky, a terrier mix, loved to go for walks with his owner. One of his favorite places to hang out was a large grassy area near a lake. He would run to the edge of the water and chase birds, then race through the tall grasses, playing hide-and-go-seek with George, his loving master. Afterward, he would go exploring, looking for adventure along the way. George always allowed Spunky this freedom for a few minutes before putting him back on the leash and the grateful pup learned to appreciate it.

On one trip to the lake, George and Spunky walked along a well-worn path. The little terrier found all sorts of things to sniff and nibble, everything from bits of old food to a worn shoe. Each item was like a gift, waiting to be unwrapped.

Then came the real treasure! A large pile of something he'd never seen before. Spunky wasn't sure what the odd stuff was—and it did have a peculiar smell—but he rolled around in it, just the same. Oh, how wonderful it felt. . .almost as nice as when George rubbed his tummy. Still, the smell was starting to get worse.

Before long, Spunky's entire coat was covered. George caught him in the act and scolded him for getting into manure—whatever that was. Within minutes, with the afternoon sunlight beaming down, the icky stuff began to harden. And man, did it ever stink! Spunky could hardly stand it. He tried rolling around in the tall grasses, but it was no use. The smell wouldn't go away. What had started as fun ended as anything but!

George pinched his nose as he walked home with Spunky at his side. As soon as they arrived home, the little terrier had a bath with lots and lots of puppy shampoo. Unfortunately the stench didn't go away, so George washed Spunky again. And again. Before long, the poor little terrier was waterlogged. Still, the odor remained. He started to wonder if it would ever go away.

Do you sometimes feel like Spunky? Maybe you're an adventurer at heart and this gets you in trouble. Perhaps, while out exploring, you stumbled upon something that looked really good at first glance. Maybe you let your guard down. Rolled around in it. At first, you probably didn't even notice the stench. You didn't realize what you'd been toying with. It didn't take long, however, before you were covered! And all of the bathing in the world wouldn't make it go away!

Sin always leaves its mark, and it's often a mark we can't hide from others. Thankfully, God sent His Son into the world for this very purpose—to cleanse us from our sins. To get rid of the mark. Through His sacrifice on the cross, He accomplished something miraculous! Jesus took every stench. . .every stain. . .and washed it all away.

A Good Shepherd?

DONNA K. MALTESE

You were continually straying like sheep, but now you have returned to the Shepherd and Guardian of your souls.
1 PETER 2:25 NASB

Every Christmas Eve, my husband, children, and I pack up the presents and, along with the family dog, head to my Italian in-laws' house where we spend the day, talking, exchanging gifts, and feasting on the requisite seven-fishes dinner.

One particular Christmas Eve, our two kids were anxious to open gifts. So, with full stomachs, we heaved away from the dining room table and waddled into the living room, with our one-year-old German-shepherd mixed mutt named Schaefer (which in Pennsylvania German means "Shepherd") trailing behind.

For a few moments, we admired my mother-in-law Lili's beautifully decorated Christmas tree and then my father-in-law Carl's pride and joy—the clay crèche (complete with manger, star, Mary, Joseph, baby Jesus, wise men, shepherds, donkey, and lamb) that he painstakingly sets up beneath the tree every year.

Soon we settled down to unwrapping presents and oohing

and aahing over each gift. During a momentary lull in the proceedings, Carl looked at his crèche and said, "Where's the donkey?" As soon as the words left his mouth, everything in the world seemed to slow down.

I scanned the room for Schaefer, then spotted him amid the wads and sheets of Christmas wrapping strewn around the room. He was chewing on something! Our eyes locked. Then in one horrifying moment, I saw something jutting from between Schaefer's jaws.

"Schaefer!" I yelled.

The pup looked stunned, his ears straight up, the donkey's leg hanging off his lower lip.

I leaped up from the organ bench and rushed to extricate from Schaefer's mouth what was left of the donkey—a leg. Just a single solitary leg.

Carl couldn't believe it! The thirty-five year-old crèche he'd carefully wrapped in tissue paper after each Christmas—its donkey ravaged in a matter of minutes by an SPCA hound! For the first time since I'd known Carl, he was speechless, utterly and profoundly speechless.

Lili immediately stepped in, trying to make light of the moment by saying, "Years later we'll laugh about it! We'll remember this Christmas as the Christmas Schaefer ate all but the donkey's leg."

Praise God for family members who make light of what can be volatile moments. And thank God for our sinless Good Shepherd who never gave in to temptation—unlike our pup, a not-so-good shepherd, who often gave in to his wolfish nature.

We humans all know the voice of our Good Shepherd—the

one who protects and provides for us. Each and every day, we make a choice. Will we listen to Jesus, following His wise counsel, or obey the voice of the stranger, give in to our wolfish nature, and stray, saying or doing things we know will displease our true Lord and Master?

Exacto Wrongo

DEE ASPIN

Do not give false testimony against your neighbor [. . .or dog!].
EXODUS 20:16 HCSB

"When I was six years old and begged for a dog, my parents bought me a chow and then returned it when it wouldn't train easily," the man with the Hawaiian shirt and Texan accent said, recalling his destiny dog, his childhood companion. "I was devastated, but they said I could get another dog. My neighbors had a poodle—somehow I decided that's what I wanted.

"This poodle, Angel, and I became very close—I loved her. She even slept on my bed," he continued, smiling.

"For years every Christmas I used to get out an Exacto knife, and the week of Christmas, after mom put the presents around the tree, I would precisely cut a little square under the bow and peek. Carefully I would replace the tissue so they would never know I looked.

"One Christmas I became too hasty and ripped the peek area. I didn't know what to do; my parents would be angry. So I made multiple rips like the size of my dog's paw so it would look like Angel did it. The next day I showed my dad and said, 'Look what Angel got into!'

"I'll never forget my dad getting angry with Angel. She was so smart. She just glared at me from across the room like she was mad at me. I could swear her look said, 'You little rat. I thought you were my friend.' Immediately I felt so guilty, like I really blew it. . .and I never did that again."

I had to grimace, recalling the guilt I felt watching my younger brother in the corner of the room with his hands up saying, "No, Mom, no!" My mom used a tiny little plastic cord that stung if it hit our arm or leg. We all hated that little thing, but it was a good nominal way to discipline us if we got out of line.

Even though I don't remember what we did to get in trouble, I do remember my older brother and I did something wrong and conspired to blame my younger brother. Both our words against his. So he got it—not us. I still remember watching him from the doorway as guilt crept over me.

I also knew one of the Ten Commandments at a very early age: Don't bear false witness against your neighbors, or your brother, or your dog. (They just might bite back.)

Lying about friends or family to get ourselves off the hook is like stealing—it robs someone's reputation. In addition, we can cause them undeserved consequences. It's like doing two wrongs at once—creating guilt. The only way to deal with it is apologize to God and those we hurt. If it's too far in the past, we may not know if we should address it.

Just recently, I had to ask forgiveness from someone who has felt slighted by me from an event ten years ago. I didn't realize something was wrong until someone else told me the person was still upset. Thank goodness from our dogs we learn that to err is human, to forgive canine.

Roy Boy and Silent Cal

DONNA K. MALTESE

[Jesus said,] "Stop judging by mere appearances,
and make a right judgment."
JOHN 7:24 NIV

In the 1960s, many families kept their dogs in the backyard, chained to a doghouse. My family did the same with a white English pointer that, oddly enough, never barked. So my parents dubbed him Calvin, after a president of few words, Calvin "Silent Cal" Coolidge. They'd brought Calvin back with them on a cross-country road trip from California to Pennsylvania, along with two little girls (both under the age of three) and all their worldly possessions. Somehow, along the way, Mom got pregnant with me. But that's a whole 'nother story.

During Calvin's reign, my father, as a joke, decided to buy his friend Roy a billy goat for his thirtieth birthday. The only problem was—where to keep it? Since we lived in town, we didn't have our own barn. So my father decided to move Calvin into our basement and chain the white billy goat, dubbed Roy Boy, to Calvin's doghouse.

In many small towns, everyone keeps an eye on the neighborhood and usually has their nose in everyone else's business. Our town was no different.

The morning after Roy Boy's arrival, a nearsighted backyard neighbor looked out her kitchen window and up at our house. To her surprise, she thought our dog Calvin had turned into a goat overnight! Mrs. N said to her husband, "The Schoelkopf's dog— he's got horns!" She dropped her curtains and ran up through the field and backyards to the doghouse where, to her terror, she saw that the barkless Calvin had indeed, apparently, turned into a full-fledged billy goat. She rushed up to our kitchen porch, breathless as she pounded on the door.

My mother answered, somewhat surprised at Mrs. N's disheveled appearance and terror-stricken face. "Mrs. N? What's wrong?" my mother asked.

"Your—your dog. It–it's got horns!"

Laughing, my mother assured Mrs. N that our hornless dog was safe in the basement, and Roy Boy the goat was only a temporary resident. An abashed Mrs. N was quite relieved and walked back to her house, chuckling at her own foolishness.

Unfortunately, Mom's assessment that Roy Boy was only a temporary boarder was wrong, as the birthday boy laughingly refused the goat as a gift, and it took Dad awhile to find him a good home on a nearby farm.

The moral of the story? Things aren't always what they seem. And many times we make rash judgments based on what we deem as "evidence" before our very eyes.

But Jesus taught us better. He told us not to make judgments on mere appearance. When we do, we will undoubtedly make errors—thinking dogs can be transformed into billy goats, seemingly overnight! So be wise: Think, and ask God to give you a clear vision, before you make any assessments. By doing so, you can oft avoid looking like a fool.

LET SLEEPING DOGS LIE: GRACE

*Well-behaved dogs take their punishment to heart,
hang their heads, and don't repeat the offense.
When we want to say "I'm sorry" and we mean it,
we shouldn't repeat the offense either.*

KATHERINE DOUGLAS

On the Run!

JANICE HANNA

"So he got up and went to his father. But while he was still a long way off, his father saw him and was filled with compassion for him; he ran to his son, threw his arms around him and kissed him."
LUKE 15:20 NIV

Molly, a miniature schnauzer, was an indoor dog. Oh, she got to play in the backyard, too; but her world, as she knew it, was the inside of the house. She had every square inch memorized. Because it was so familiar, she often felt a little bored. She wondered if she might be missing out on something bigger, grander.

Oftentimes Molly would watch as Gillian, her owner, would open the front door and head off to some unknown place. That door began to represent freedom to Molly. She made a vow that one day she would go through it and explore the world on the other side.

Sure enough, the following week she spied an opportunity. Just as Gillian came in, Molly shot out. . .fast as you please! Once outside, she marveled at what she saw! Houses, cars, and people abounded. She began to run, run, run, more excited than ever. Oh, the possibilities! Off in the distance, she heard her master's voice calling, but Molly refused to turn around. Not now! Not when she was having such a blast!

Before long, she was on the sidewalk, chasing a boy with a ball. The fun continued as Molly saw a pile of leaves. She jumped in them and they scattered. The wind picked up several of them and blew them into the street. Molly ran after them, determined to catch one in her teeth. Oh, what fun!

Suddenly, she heard a terrible noise. The squeal of tires! A honking horn! Seconds later, a car loomed over her. Yikes! She'd almost been hit. Molly rushed to the side of the road, panting. The man in the car got out and started hollering at her. Then, as her master came running, the man yelled at *her*, too. Molly couldn't stop shaking.

A wave of relief washed over her as Gillian reached down and scooped her into her arms, speaking words of love over her. The mean man in the car took off and they were left alone. Molly gave Gillian a hundred kisses on her cheeks and promised never to run off again.

Have you ever felt like Molly? Maybe you've walked with God for years and lived an obedient life. But, like that curious puppy, you wondered what was on the other side of the door. Perhaps the desire to "explore" became too strong, so you wandered away, finding many adventures and exciting things to do. Things that seemed harmless.

And then. . .the squeal of tires. Honking horns. You stumbled into a situation that put your life—physically or symbolically speaking—in danger. Suddenly, things were spiraling out of control. Everything—and everyone—turned against you.

Oh, the joy of knowing the Father waits with arms extended for us to turn back to Him! He longs for you to come back to the safety of His embrace. Today, relish the love of your heavenly Father as He welcomes you back home.

Dumping Old Baggage

KATHERINE DOUGLAS

Let us strip off everything that hinders us, as well as the sin which dogs our feet, and let us run the race that we have to run with patience, our eyes fixed on Jesus the source and the goal of our faith.
HEBREWS 12:1–2 PHILLIPS

It all began when he was a puppy.

Kendall's German shorthair, Lucky, developed an attachment to a teddy bear. In the house, Lucky carries Teddy around from room to room unless something else has his undivided attention. Even though Teddy is roughly the same size as Lucky, Lucky holds on to the stuffed bear with the tenacity of a pit bull. When it's bedtime, Lucky wraps his paws around his teddy bear and snuggles in for the night. Lucky would no sooner sleep without his Teddy than Linus of *Peanuts* cartoon fame would be without his blankie. Lucky must follow only one rule: The teddy bear stays in the house. He isn't allowed to drag his bedtime buddy out in the dirt.

That's why Kendall was puzzled one day when she saw Lucky carting his teddy bear around the yard—or what she thought was his teddy bear. To Kendall's horror, the brown furry thing Lucky had in his paws wasn't his teddy bear. Lucky had killed a groundhog. He wasn't about to part with the dead baggage. He was cuddling up to his quarry just like he did to Teddy. Gagging and grumbling, Kendall managed to get Lucky away from the groundhog so she could clean up Lucky. She left the uglier deed—the burial of Teddy's dead twin, the groundhog—to her husband.

Not much time passed. Again Kendall noticed that Lucky wasn't running around the yard much.

It couldn't be, could it?

Ugh! Not again!

Lucky had dug up the dead groundhog and was carting it around the yard. Now the mess was worse. Lucky was snuggling up with the dirtied, bloodied, and dried-up, dog-drool-covered, deceased groundhog. Kendall nearly lost it—again.

For round two, she gave not-so-Lucky his second bath of the day—not to mention a second shower for herself. Kendall's husband took care to dig a deeper hole outside their yard, for what they hoped would be the groundhog's final resting place. They both breathed a sigh of relief when the second "planting" worked.

We don't have to carry around, or be weighted down by, the dead deeds of our past. Our own consciences—or even other people—can dig up our past sins and load us down with guilt. But if we have received Christ and trust in Him, we've been released from sin's hold on us (see Romans 8:1–2). Jesus forgives us. He frees us from the baggage of our past. We don't need to dig it up.

Jesus dealt with our sin at the cross. The Lord has separated us from the dead deeds of our past, just as Kendall separated Lucky from the unfortunate groundhog. And as Lucky was clean after his super scrubbing, so has our Savior thoroughly washed us up and readied us to go on.

With the dead groundhog finally laid to rest, Lucky stayed free—and clean—of his groundhog baggage. Thanks to the Lord Jesus, and with all of heaven cheering us on (see Hebrews 12:1), we're clean and baggage-free, too!

trouble with truffles

MILLIE MCCLOY

Therefore, as the elect of God, holy and beloved, put on tender mercies,
kindness, humility, meekness, longsuffering; bearing with one another,
and forgiving one another, if anyone has a complaint against another;
even as Christ forgave you, so you also must do. But above all these
things put on love, which is the bond of perfection.
COLOSSIANS 3:12–14 NKJV

With a wistful look and a wagging tail, Truffles leaned heavily into the screened door. Karen was outside—just a few leaps away—arranging flowers in her new perennial bed. Beside her lay a large bag of potting soil and an assortment of colorful young flowers and pots. Truffles watched Karen carefully dig each hole, place a plant, and shovel dirt. He was not at all sure what Karen was doing, but it sure looked like fun.

Karen worked outside for a long time, silently ignoring the whining and wincing of her English sheepdog. Truffles eventually turned from the door and shuffled over to his bowl. He would comfort himself with the last tidbits of doggie doodle donuts—his favorite.

Later that afternoon when Karen had finished her shower, she answered Truffles audible "out" plea without hesitation as she had done hundreds of times before. With a gentle push on the screened door she turned Truffles outside.

It wasn't until early evening, as Karen began preparing dinner, that she remembered Truffles was still outside and had made no effort to call for entry. *This can't be good,* thought Karen.

Karen walked over to the door, stepped out, and quickly scanned the yard for her dog. At that same moment Truffles came bounding down the walk toward Karen. If dogs could smile, Truffles was grinning from ear to ear! Potting soil was all over the sidewalk, all over Truffles, and all over his face and paws. Plants and pots were everywhere—everywhere but where they had been placed. The garden had been leveled, and in the middle of the soil, Truffles had dug himself a sizable arena. He barked excitedly, inviting Karen to his new playground.

Tears flooded Karen's face, and anger overcame her. She yelled at Truffles and, without thought, lunged at him. In that particular instant of time, Karen caught her sandal on the trowel that had been misplaced on the sidewalk. It was not a pretty fall, and certainly not an easy one. Before Truffles could flee from his master, Karen flipped a somersault and landed with her face at Truffles' feet, sunny side down. Karen lay still for what seemed like a very long time. Although she felt like crying uncontrollably for the loss of her beautiful masterpiece, her garden, and for the pain she was now in, she suddenly found herself laughing hysterically. Truffles, too, was quite amused and began rolling once again in the fresh dirt surrounding them both.

Karen reached over and gently pulled Truffles to her. She embraced him, dirt and all. She loved that pup. Forgiveness came quickly.

My Day in Dog Court

SHELLEY LEE

He will judge the world in righteousness;
he will govern the peoples with justice.
PSALM 9:8 NIV

I was sitting next to a handcuffed man in a stuffy courtroom filled with repeat offenders and various lawbreakers. Awaiting my turn, I heard story after sordid story—some more colorful than others—brought before the judge. Finally my case was called and I made my way through the waiting, captive crowd to the bench.

"What can I do for you?" asked the judge.

A silence hung for a moment or two before I replied, "My dog crossed the road, sir."

I can only imagine how many furrowing eyebrows and laughing eyes I'd have met had I been audacious enough not to give my attention to the judge.

See, some months earlier, the dog warden was called to the scene of a mysterious reported dog crossing.

We were not home when the now-loathed maroon extended van, with a threatening display of unlit yellow lights, tracked down the owners registered to the dog's tag. She was found suspect, caught red-pawed, hanging out with the neighbors across the street, who loved her but were not willing to claim her—hence, pay her fine. She was cuffed, clown-collared, and hauled off to the pound.

I arrived home from work to find four hungry children, their homework assignments, and a notice stuck to the front door. The dog warden, apparently very irritated, skipped right over a ticketed fine to a court order, along with the daily rates the pound charges to keep offenders such as ours.

With less than an hour before the jail fees doubled, my husband hurried over to retrieve our frightened four-legged criminal. There, he paid more than what a night at a cheap motel might cost, for bail. He was also made aware that it is a crime to want your dog to have a litter of puppies.

The warden, who insisted on being called "officer," informed him that there was an extra charge for not having spayed the dog. It's a good thing the warden was not the judge, or he would have held us in contempt! There was the issue of not properly addressing him, an apparent superior. . .over dogs. And there was our questioning of the freedom to responsibly have puppies—how dare we!

In the end, the case was dismissed, we paid the court fees, and chalked it up as a great 125-dollar story that makes people laugh every time. Yet, as I think about the bigger lessons here, I am grateful that God is indeed a righteous Judge who rules with wisdom, love, and grace. He is without question, a superior worthy of the respect due His many titles. He does not hold me in contempt; rather He knows my lowly state and still hears my plea. He also has a marvelous sense of humor and likely had a good, hearty laugh over my day in dog court.

Samson and DeRopa

DEE ASPIN

And as we live in God, our love grows more perfect. So we will not be afraid on the day of judgement, but we can face him with confidence because we live like Jesus here in this world.

1 JOHN 4:17 NLT

You know Sam's cage in the corner of the yard?" my friend said on the phone. "I put him in it this morning because the pool guy was coming. Well, today Sam broke out and escaped!"

I pictured her golden retriever and the twelve-by-six cyclone fence and chuckled.

"I grabbed his twenty-five-foot-long leash," Beth continued, "and attached it to the kennel so he could still go in and out." Her children giggled in the background. "I gave him dog treats, water with ice cubes, planted an umbrella for him to lounge under, and set him up nicely. Then I joined the pool man at the other side of the yard.

"So we're standing there talking about the pool, and we both looked up at the same time. Along comes Sam padding up to join us with a shredded rope hanging from his neck!" She laughed lightly.

"Well, I wasn't real happy at the moment, so I pointed back to his little piece of paradise and said, 'Samson, get back.'

"The pool man looked at me and asked, 'Samson? Get off! Really?'

" 'Yes, his name is Samson,' I affirmed.

"He looked at me, eyes wide, and grinned from ear to ear. 'You mean his name is Samson and you tried to secure him with a rope? Maybe you should cut his hair so he isn't so strong.' "

Beth laughed exuberantly, highly amused when she connected the dots. And because of her amusement, Samson got off the hook for his escape.

Sometimes we don't see the humor when our critters are behaving badly—or even the big or little people in our lives. When we have done all we can to make their lives easier and they are still restless and doing crazy things, maybe it helps to remember we have our moments, too.

Aren't we all a little bit like Samson?

Have you ever tried to do the right thing, like getting to work on time, but went about it the wrong way—by speeding? Have you ever been stopped for a traffic ticket and said something that made the officer laugh and he let you off? (Like Samson was a rope-breaker, so we are lawbreakers.)

"Okay," says the officer, "this time is a warning, but next time you may not be so lucky. Be careful."

Why does the officer let us go? Because we eased his tension. We made him laugh, and humor makes everyone feel better. Humor always helps. The Bible says laughter is like good medicine (see Proverbs 17:22).

Maybe today we can bestow grace rather than confront someone who sent another questionable e-mail or left a dirty mug in the sink at work. Instead of making an issue of a trespass, if we can find humor in it—turn it to a positive.

Possibly we can remember times God has been patient with us and given us a break because He knows who we are inside and out, bad moments and good, and still loves us anyhow.

Laughter and Canine Chaos

SHELLEY LEE

*A happy heart is good medicine and a cheerful mind works healing,
but a broken spirit dries up the bones.*

PROVERBS 17:22 AMP

Our loving shepherd-Lab, Zoey, has a servant's heart. That's what I told myself every time I'd load the dishwasher and she was immediately there, licking rinsed silverware right on to the floor. It was annoying, but if I reminded myself that she thought she was helping, it didn't bother me as much. Even though the truth was probably that she was bored drinking water out of the same old bowl all the time. Licking it off eating surfaces was much more fun!

One evening like any other, I was loading the dishes while two of my sons, Mitch and Wes, were in the kitchen, making a sandwich and reading mail, respectively. While the boys and I chatted about the events of the day, Zoey was at her post by my side, head poised over the sliding bottom basket that was pulled out, getting filled with dishes, pans, and silverware.

She rested her neck on the edge of the sturdy sliding basket, leaned slightly inward, straining for more drips of water, and suddenly she panicked beyond reason.

The moment I realized that her collar was caught on the basket was the same nanosecond the kitchen seemed to explode in one fluid motion. The crashing noise hit my senses before the flash of flying dishes, glass, and metal, followed by Zoey attached to a large dish basket with small wheels, followed by a portable island on big wheels getting pulled into the melee, pitching forward with its shelves of breakable contents looking to be a part of the excitement.

All powered by panic and lack of understanding (both common for Zoey).

We stood there stunned for half a second before I yelled to Mitch, closest to the dog, "Grab Zoey!" who was still in motion. Wes simultaneously caught the island on wheels before it crashed over. Zoey broke free from the heavy metal basket, which she probably thought had attacked her, and she fled the scene in fear.

"What just happened?" Wes said, more as a statement than a question.

His youngest brother Dexter, running in to see what all the commotion was about, found us all standing still, surrounded by shards of glass, forks, knives, bowls, and the second broken Corelle dish in fifteen years. But let me tell you—when they break, they really break; we're talking jagged daggers. But no one was hurt.

We all just started laughing hysterically. Zoey peeked around the corner as if asking if the attack basket had left yet. "Is it safe to return?" her eyes asked.

We worked together to clear paths for each other, laughing all along as we slowly cleaned up the unusual mess and retold the story to Dexter and then Dad when he got home, then later on the phone to the oldest brother, Trevor, away at college. Laughing again.

I later thought how grateful I am that we found the humor in that, instead of the inconvenience. How a few broken dishes are a small price to pay to find happy hearts in one of the many messes of life.

We've laughed many times since. Zoey, however, prefers now to drink her water out of the same old bowl, or the cat's bowl, but that's another story.

A "tail" of Durham-the-Doggedly-Determined-Destroyer

DONNA K. MALTESE

*The LORD is my strength and my shield; my heart trusts in him,
and I am helped. My heart leaps for joy and
I will give thanks to him in song.*

PSALM 28:7 NIV

My "tail" begins when, after a long and arduous search for a healthy canine, God blessed my family with a puppy named Durham. He is a shar-pei–yellow Lab mix that has more energy than a category-5 hurricane, as evidenced by three ravaged tennis balls, ten holes in the backyard (there's a mole in there somewhere), one now-deformed lilac bush, a neighbor's ruined Christmas stocking, seven ripped up socks, three shredded books (one of which was, ironically enough, entitled *The Curious Incident of the Dog in the Night-Time*), one broken leash, three chewed up baskets, at least two missing refrigerator magnets, a tossed-into-the-oven-then-melted SuperBall, and, well, you get the general idea. With this latest addition to our family, the bizarre has become routine.

One night, my husband and I joined forces and pushed a snoring, restless-leg-syndrome Durham out of our bed. An hour later, I was awakened by a spasmodically jolting mattress. Yes, Durham—back on the covers again—was now in the throes of a violent hiccupping spell. We once more shoved the mutt off our bed before drifting off to what little sleep we could garner before another round of bestial canine snoring began.

Since that night, Durham has grown to a solid ninety-pound mass of muscle that takes my husband and me for regular walks. He continues to teethe on rawhide bones, his dog cushion, our bedroom's Berber carpet, and, on occasion, my grandmother's upholstered rocking chair. And there are still occasional surprises, like when I came out of my home office one day, opened the door to the upstairs landing, and found bits of mortar, chewed up drywall, and a rather large splintered piece of wood on our burgundy carpet. After giving an outraged cry of "Durrrhhhaaammm!!!" I recovered my senses and my peace, and thought, *Hmmm. Wonder what part of the house this came off of?* (We never did discover its original source.)

Yes, we have a healthy, loving, can't-leave-home-without-him-or-you-may-not-have-a-home-to-come-back-to dog named Durham the Destroyer. And, yes, he is a tremendous amount of work, but we do not labor in vain, for in return for our efforts, our patience, our diligence, and our tolerance, Durham gives us tremendous amounts of love and affection (when he licks our faces), joy and laughter (when he barks at his reflection in the oven door or chases his tail), comfort and warmth (when he snuggles by our side or sits *on* our feet). Besides, he's giving us ample opportunity to practice forgiveness, seven times seventy (see Matthew 18:22).

So, in the midst of the reign of Durham-the-Doggedly-Determined-Destroyer, we are experiencing joy amid the storm.

And in this we rejoice, as we do when we come out of the cold, bleak winter and into the warm sunshine of spring; when we come out of the emptiness of trusting ourselves to the fullness of faith in God; when we come out of a time of trial and into a time of blessing.

Grace in the Slippery Place

DEE ASPIN

I waited patiently for the LORD; he turned to me and heard my cry. He lifted me out of the slimy pit, out of the mud and mire; he set my feet on a rock and gave me a firm place to stand.

PSALM 40:1–2 NIV

One day I drove Hannah to the river so she could run around. Because she is a water dog, I enjoy watching her play in the California lakes and rivers almost as much as she enjoys lapping up and jumping in the water. At one point, we found a pristine water hole surrounded by big boulders off a secluded side road.

Twice before on hikes, I'd watched Hannah bound exuberantly into unknown terrain and get stuck. Once I had to beckon two male strangers to help me get her out of a crevice. She looked up at us through fiery black eyes from the grassy dirt pit twelve feet below—barking wildly. I couldn't help but laugh.

On this particular day, I sat squarely on the flat surface of a large boulder, watching her from across the pool. Hannah looked down at the tempting water from the circle of rocks surrounding the cool river reservoir. Would she really jump into that liquid trap surrounded by four feet of slippery, wet boulders? Had she learned her lesson from the last two fiascos?

Sure enough, Hannah stared longingly at the glistening mirror beneath her and carefully slid her muscular, black body slowly down the side of the smooth, wet granite. She swam calmly, enjoying herself. I waited and watched—smiling. Soon, her eyes began to widen as she paddled to one boulder, then another, attempting to position her paws on each rock for leverage to hoist herself up...but quickly slipping back into the pool each time.

Her panting increased as her eyes riveted to each of the boulders encircling her. The rocks stood like expressionless, unsympathetic sentries—silent immovable witnesses of her leisurely swim that had transformed into a terrible trap. Their cold, hard faces offered no relief as Hannah moved from rock to rock to rock, only to slide and slide and slide back down. Finally, she paddled over to me and looked up, pleading with her eyes. *Help!*

Laughing, I jumped in and stood in four feet of water. She placed her back legs on my thighs and sprang to safety. I knew all along the predictable ending to her curious beginning.

I think God is like that. He already knows He'll be reaching out His hand to help us up when we begin to sink from our ridiculous plights—the ones we get ourselves into.

I'm so glad He's there, with us, even in the middle of our predicaments—as soon as we get anxious and realize we have made a mistake. And even if we don't turn to Him right away, instead leaning on our own strength and useless efforts, still He watches and waits. As soon as we turn to Him, He stretches out His hand and does whatever we need to plant us on solid ground...once again.

Dressed. . .from the Inside Out

JANICE HANNA

*"And why worry about a speck in your friend's
eye when you have a log in your own?"*
LUKE 6:41 NLT

Angel was a two-year-old Chihuahua with a bit of an attitude problem. She had a tendency to snap at people, and usually when they least expected it. Fortunately. . .or unfortunately. . .Angel belonged to Donna, a woman who let her get away with anything and everything. Talk about spoiled! If Angel made a mess, Donna cleaned it up without scolding. If the dog snapped at the neighbors, Donna made excuses.

Despite her mean-spirited nature, Angel was often dressed in adorable little doggie outfits and sparkling collars. Donna particularly loved putting her pup in a precious angel costume. Others saw the irony but not Donna. Oh no. She would take the ornery pup into public to show off the costume. Folks passing by would see her and *ooh* and *ahh*. Many would make the mistake of reaching out to pet her as they carried on about how darling she was. They learned very quickly that Angel was no angel. A little demon was more like it. Unfortunately, a couple of folks learned this too late, after she snapped at them.

After an episode where Angel bit a neighbor, Donna finally realized the error of her ways and signed the naughty pup up for obedience training. Though it took a considerable amount of work, the little beast was finally tamed. Before long her insides matched her outside. She could wear that angel costume. . .and mean it.

Sometimes people are a lot like Angel. . .all dolled up on the outside, putting forth a near-perfect image. They want others to see only the good and not the bad. However, their true colors shine through when you bump up against them. This is even true of church folks. (*Gasp!*) Sometimes believers work extra hard to put forth a good image, concerned about how they are viewed by others. Then something happens and they get riled up. . .and watch out! The inside doesn't match the outside anymore!

So, where do you stand? Are you really who you say you are, who you present yourself to be? Or have you—especially among your Christian peers—started to put on a front because you're afraid to let people see the real you? Are you worried they won't like what they see if you let your guard down or stop pretending?

It's time to get honest. Real. If you're struggling with an internal problem like anger or jealousy, allow the Lord to heal you from the inside out. Let Him peel back the facade and do a true, intimate work. He longs to see you healed and whole. And look on the bright side—once His work is done, you won't have to plaster on a smile. The joy will bubble up naturally! Talk about being dressed from the inside out!

THE BIG DOGS: GOD'S PROTECTION

It's funny how dogs and cats know the inside of folks better than other folks do, isn't it?

ELEANOR H. PORTER

Run to the Battle

JANICE HANNA

*So that we may boldly say, The Lord is my helper,
and I will not fear what man shall do unto me.*
HEBREWS 13:6 KJV

Some dogs are bolder by nature than others, and some love to yap more than others. Such was the case with Sasha, a thirteen-pound red doxie (aka, dachsund). A city dog at heart, she hardly knew what do with herself when her owner, Annie, took her to the country for a couple of days. Suddenly the entire landscape of her existence changed. Instead of concrete sidewalks, postage-stamp lawns, and suburban houses, Sasha was introduced to wide open fields, barns, and tractors. The most interesting thing of all? The tall, four-legged creatures in the pasture. Horses.

When Sasha heard them whinnying, she felt sure they were set to attack. The bold doxie flew into action to protect her owner from these strange, elusive creatures. Now, she'd never been introduced to a horse before, but the sheer size of the magnificent beasts didn't scare her. . .not from a distance, anyway. No, sir. She ran full steam ahead, yapping all the way. Her plan? To bite them in the ankles. To protect her owner from harm!

Only one problem. The closer she got to them, they bigger they appeared! And, as Sasha drew near, the horse in the front began to take several rapid steps toward her. Yikes! She had never planned on a counterattack! Fear took hold and she stopped in her tracks. It was one thing to run after him; another altogether to have *him* run after her!

Sasha began to take several steps backward, rethinking her plan. All of her boldness slipped away in an instant as the monster made his way toward her. Before long, she turned and ran, praying all the while that her enemy would not follow. Thankfully, he stopped after just a few steps. From that day forth, she would cower every time she saw horses nearby. Their very presence intimidated her.

Have you walked a mile in Sasha's paws? Can you relate? Sometimes life presents us with extreme obstacles and we run boldly toward them, ready to conquer them head-on. Fear never enters into it. Pure adrenaline drives us forward. Then, as we get closer, we begin to feel threatened. Our boldness slips away. We cower in fear.

Today, the Lord wants to remind you that no matter how big your problem might be, He is bigger still. No matter how tall the mountain, He can move it. Even the most "magnificent beast" is tiny in His sight. So, don't let the enemy call your bluff. Don't back down. Instead, run with confidence, knowing the Lord is right there with you, giving you the boldness you need to see things through.

A Brave Guard Dog

RACHEL QUILLIN

The wicked flee when no man pursueth:
but the righteous are bold as a lion.
PROVERBS 28:1 KJV

Seth poured a cup of coffee and began to eat his cereal when a familiar noise greeted his ears. Annoyed by the early morning disturbance, he went to the kitchen window.

"Hush, Snickers!" he yelled to the border collie. The dog ceased his barking only long enough to glance up at his master. Then, as if to say, "I'll do what I want," Snickers turned back to the rabbit that had captured his attention. The barking was renewed with greater intensity. Seth watched as Snickers tugged at his chain, trying to reach the rabbit. Suddenly the rabbit hopped too close to Snickers. Inwardly Seth cheered the dog on, willing the animal to do what came instinctively to his kind. But he shook his head as the dog tucked his tail and hurried to his doghouse.

"Big, brave dog," he muttered. It had been the same since Snickers was a puppy. Seth had played and worked with the dog, but Snickers feared even his own shadow. Groundhogs, birds, cats—it didn't matter. They all made Snickers more than a little uncomfortable, and the truth was, they were all safe in his presence. The rabbits began to recognize this pattern and didn't bother to be afraid of their natural enemy. They knew his bark would cause them no harm.

As Christians, God instills a boldness in us that even our natural enemies can't penetrate. Though these foes might appear larger than life and quite fearsome, their power only runs so deep.

As we walk with God more and more each day, we begin to recognize just how superficial the bark of the dog is. Like David as he faced Goliath, we know that the God we serve is bigger than any dog or giant or any other unrighteous enemy we will ever face.

Satan will do all that he can to torment us, but God is in control. Like Christ, we, too, can say, "Get thee behind me, Satan" (Matthew 16:23 KJV). In Ephesians 6:13–18, the apostle Paul reminds us of the spiritual armor that we are to put on. Not one item covers our back. That shows us that, just like the rabbits in Snickers' presence, we have no reason for retreat. We stand up to our enemies because it's really God who, through all of these means, fights our battles for us. We will face enemies. We will find ourselves in the heat of battle, but we will find ourselves victorious. "The righteous *are* bold as a lion" (Proverbs 28:1 KJV, emphasis added), and it is the wicked who will have to retreat.

We need to be careful not to become arrogant in our spirituality, though. What if just one time, Snickers actually would attack? The rabbits and birds would be easily defeated by him. That's what happens when we play too closely around temptation. God does give us boldness to stand up to the enemy, but He also gives us wisdom to know where we need to set boundaries. If we don't follow God's limits, we take the chance of falling into the enemy's trap. So while we should be bold, we also must remember that all of our victories are through the strength of God.

the Enemy

MARILEE PARRISH

*Be self-controlled and alert. Your enemy the devil prowls
around like a roaring lion looking for someone to devour.*
1 PETER 5:8 NIV

Jodi's dog, Max, was a small Yorkshire terrier. Max was a tiny little thing but could be very aggressive when he wanted to be. Max didn't care much for strangers. He didn't like the mailman, and he threw a fit when anyone stuck a pamphlet in the door. And when out-of-town guests came to visit, it took the little dog days to warm up. But Max's mortal enemy was the vacuum cleaner. Max hated the vacuum with a passion and would attack the contraption on sight. Jodi stored the vacuum in the closet and dreaded the weekly cleaning when Max and the vacuum would battle "to the death." Jodi always tried to vacuum the carpets when Max was busy with other things or playing in the backyard with his favorite ball. But as soon as Max would hear the vacuum's hideous voice, he would race inside to protect his home from the ferocious monster.

Max would jump on the vacuum, scratching it and pawing at it through the entire length of the house. He would squeal and yelp, demanding that the beast give up and go back to his hideout. Max always seemed to win the fight. By the time Jodi had finished cleaning the downstairs, Max was hoarse, but the vacuum stopped and went back to wherever it came from. Max felt victorious every time.

One morning during a particularly vicious battle between the dog and his enemy, Jodi remembered that she had left a pot boiling on the stove. Without shutting off the vacuum, she ran to the kitchen to tend to the pot. Max was momentarily distracted, watching his master run off. Not paying attention to what was happening, Max looked around the corner to see what Jodi was doing. He backed right into the vacuum extension, which immediately grabbed his long hair and sucked him in. The vacuum was winning. Max was stuck. He could not get the machine to let go of his hair. He yipped and yelped for help. Jodi heard the struggle and came to Max's rescue. She turned off the vacuum, and Max ran for cover.

First Corinthians 10:12 (NIV) says that "if you think you are standing firm, be careful that you don't fall." In other words, don't ever think you are so strong that you can't be shaken. You just might get knocked down a few pegs! Just like the vacuum, the devil is always watching and waiting for us to trip up. He wants us to be momentarily distracted so he can swoop in and catch us off guard. But if we keep our eyes on Jesus at all times, the devil doesn't stand a chance.

When the Lion King Shows Up

CHUCK MILLER

If you make the Most High your dwelling—even the LORD, who is my refuge—then no harm will befall you, no disaster will come near your tent. For he will command his angels concerning you, to guard you in all your ways; they will lift you up in their hands, so that you will not strike your foot against a stone. You will tread upon the lion and the cobra.

PSALM 91:9–13 NIV

Okay, so this is a dog-*and*-cat story. But the dog is the key, obviously, as you will see.

We have a gray inside-outside cat named Baby, and a giant (as our vet calls him) collie named Symba. Yes, we named him after the chief character from *The Lion King*, whom he does resemble.

We live on a street that dead-ends at a bluff leading down to a creek. It's not some nature-lover's dream. . .just a weedy little bluff leading down to a weedy little creek in the little city of Toledo, Ohio. It is nice to live on a dead-end street. However, this bluff does harbor some unsavory characters.

One afternoon as I was walking Symba before I left for work, I heard a cat hissing down by the bluff, sounding like the steam-pipes in my grandparents' basement. As Symba and I approached, we saw Baby facing off along the edge of the bluff with a raccoon about three times his size. Standing nearly fifteen feet apart, the cat was hissing, and there was a rumble coming from the chest of the raccoon.

As we walked, Symba approached this scene with the same attitude he has toward every situation he approaches: "Hey, you know, this might turn out to be fun!" And he's smiling his collie smile, you know. . .showing his teeth.

The raccoon took a long look at Symba—or, more accurately, I suppose at those teeth—stopped rumbling, then took off like a scalded cat through the underbrush. Baby stood transfixed. He stared for a moment at the place where the raccoon had been, then looked at the dog, then back where the raccoon had been, then back at Symba. It was clear that Baby knew exactly what had just happened. Then Baby followed us up the other side of the street.

This happened twice in one workweek, in the same area down by the creek. Since that time, whenever I'm walking Symba, Baby walks with us. He'll go a little ahead, or drop a little behind, or explore up by a house or behind a house. But thirty seconds later, there the gray cat is, catching up with us, yakking nonstop at us about something or other. Occasionally, the neighbors will come out on their porches to watch the show.

You might say that for Baby, Symba is a Presence. Just like our Lord is the Presence that protects us from all harm. Since that time, Baby has gotten in some more fights, but only when he's without his protector, Symba.

that I Didn't Know Was There

CHUCK MILLER

*We have escaped like a bird out of the fowler's snare; the snare has been
broken, and we have escaped. Our help is in the name of the LORD,
the Maker of heaven and earth.*
PSALM 124:7–8 NIV

My wife and I had driven from Toledo to Myrtle Beach to be with her mom and dad while her dad was dying of cancer. After he died, our two sons drove down for the funeral, bringing Symba, our eight-month-old collie. We had moved Mom's planter stands from in front of her never-used sliding patio door so we could open it and let some fresh air in; it was December, clear, and in the 70s. Mom was in the shower.

Symba noticed that my older son was in Mom's backyard, passing time by practicing his golf swing. Symba perked up, got an idea, and like a bullet ran right through the screen door—as though the screen wasn't even there! He just wanted to be with his boy!

My wife, my younger son, and I stared at each other wide-eyed as the torn screen flapped in the breeze and young Symba danced around his boy in the backyard. Then we broke up laughing while we tried to figure out what to do!

My wife ran for Mom's sewing kit, got some black thread, and I sewed the screen back together, then we moved the planter stands back in front of the door to hide the tear until I could replace the screen. Fortunately, Mom took a long shower. But she never did understand why we four occasionally broke out in snickers on such a solemn occasion.

Back in 1973, I was nineteen, working second shift at a factory. I was a new Christian, and I had learned that I should do my "work . . .as unto the Lord" (Colossians 3:23 ASV). I worked steadily and conscientiously; when the company installed a fancy new machine, they assigned me to it to set the rate of how many pieces should be completed during a shift. After a week they set the rate, which my friends in the department thought was reasonable. I also heard that a couple guys thought it was too high, which I figured would happen. Even so, I was about to drive straight through a screen of anger, an obstacle that I didn't know was there, just as my collie would later run straight through a real screen that he didn't know was there.

A few nights after the rate was set, my old car had a hard time starting after work, and it chugged a little at stoplights during the twelve-mile commute through my hometown of Detroit. Then, as I approached home, I noticed the headlights were dimming, too. I just wanted to get home and sleep!

When I got up the next morning, I opened the hood: Someone had cut the fan belt and blocked the air filter with tar. Someone was angry over that rate. Real angry. If I had known what he or she had done, I never would have tried to drive my car. The saboteur had obviously figured the auto would quit somewhere in Detroit, at midnight. And it probably should have.

But that person didn't figure on God. And now I look back on two escapes. . .with a smile.

A Hiding Place

MariLee Parrish

You are my hiding place; you will protect me from
trouble and surround me with songs of deliverance.
Psalm 32:7 niv

A lot of dogs aren't afraid of anything. Or so it seems. But even though Jake would have protected his master from just about anything, he was afraid of lightning. Anytime there was a storm overhead, Jake would scurry inside and find a safe hiding place. Whenever the thunder rolled and the lightning struck, Jake would cower in fear, whimpering and shivering nervously until the storm was over.

After a long day at work, Jake's master, Sarah, stood by the exit, trying to muster the courage to run out into the rain. She was disappointed when she realized that she had left her umbrella in the car. Shielding her head with a magazine, Sarah hurried to her car and started home. Twenty minutes later, she pulled into the garage and ran into the house to find Jake. She knew he would be scared to death because this storm was unusually strong and loud. Jake wasn't in his usual hiding spot, so Sarah searched the house. He wasn't under the bed, he wasn't in the bathtub, and he wasn't hiding behind the couch. Sarah was getting worried, so she went to the kitchen to grab the phone and call the neighbor. That's when she saw the mess.

Every pot, pan, and storage container she owned was scattered on the kitchen floor. The cookie sheets were under the refrigerator. Her mixer was lying sideways next to her antique cookie jar. Even her old toaster, the one she hadn't seen in years and kept in the back of the cupboard, was lying haphazardly on the floor. Sarah opened the cupboard door where the pots and pans should have been and found Jake. He had removed everything from the cupboard and found a safer hiding place. Sarah chuckled at the dog, helped him out of the cupboard, and held him on the kitchen floor until the storm subsided.

God's Word tells us that "perfect love drives out fear" (1 John 4:18 NIV). When Sarah opened the cupboard and held her dog during the storm, his fear went away. His master was loving him and protecting him. We all have so many fears. Some are even paralyzing. Our heavenly Father wants to be our hiding place. No matter what you are facing, His arms are open wide and He is always willing to hold you during the storm.

Calling His Bluff

JANICE HANNA

Be self-controlled and alert. Your enemy the devil prowls around like a roaring lion looking for someone to devour. Resist him, standing firm in the faith, because you know that your brothers throughout the world are undergoing the same kind of sufferings.

1 PETER 5:8–9 NIV

Steve loved his English bulldog, Rocky. The little guy was feisty and fun. They did most everything together. . .played Frisbee, went for rides in the car, and hung out at the dog park. In short, they made a great pair.

Only one problem. Rocky loved to bark. And bark. And bark. Steve lived in an apartment, so he continually worried that the neighbors would be bothered by his best friend's need to yap. He tried everything to get the barking under control, but nothing seemed to work.

One day, things went from bad to worse. Steve was watching television when a commercial came on, one that included a ringing doorbell sound. Rocky, thinking someone was at the door, went crazy! The barking began in earnest now. The anxious pup ran straight to the door and sat there with an expectant look on his face, carrying on with a vengeance. It took several minutes to finally get him calmed down.

The first time it happened, Steve found it funny. And the second. After that, however, it started to get old. And noisy. Seemed like every time the commercial came on, Rocky—completely bluffed— would flip out. Steve did his best to mute the television whenever he noticed the commercial but didn't always catch it in time. And even though he tried to convince Rocky they weren't under attack, the yapping continued. Before long, the neighbors were complaining and Steve was about to snap. But what could he do?

We're a lot like Rocky sometimes. We think we're under attack when the enemy is really just bluffing. We react. . .in a loud, frantic way, coming unglued. . .over nothing. False alarms send us running hither, thither, and yon, and we waste time and energy getting upset over something that poses no real threat. We worry about unseen things and unknown outcomes, when all the while the Lord asks us to trust.

When was the last time someone—or something—called your bluff? How did you respond? Did you knee-jerk? Overreact? Find yourself with a mess to clean up afterward? The Bible says that the devil goes around like a roaring lion seeking someone to devour. Most of the time his roar is contrived. His bag of tricks is empty. Not realizing that, we let fear kick in or anxiety take over.

It's time for a change of plans. A new tactic. The next time you think you're under attack, take a deep breath. Don't overreact. Remember, the enemy has no real power over you. Resist him and stand firm, but don't get worked up. After all, you have the Lord Jesus Christ on your side, and the devil is no match for Him. So don't give in! Call his bluff. . .then get on with the business of living.

MAN'S BEST FRIEND:
FRIENDSHIP

*The reason a dog has so many friends is
that he wags his tail instead of his tongue.*

UNKNOWN

Closer than a Brother

MariLee Parrish

A man of many companions may come to ruin,
but there is a friend who sticks closer than a brother.
Proverbs 18:24 niv

Laddy, a beautiful and loyal collie, was a friend to the entire family but was particularly fond of the second child named Kenny. Laddy and twelve-year-old Kenny were inseparable. They grew up together and shared just about everything.

Laddy was even allowed to share Kenny's cereal. Kenny would take a bite with the spoon and then Laddy would have a lick out of the bowl. When things were hard at school or the house had too many people in it, Laddy and Kenny would head outside and have a talk. Laddy could always sense Kenny's mood. If Kenny was happy, Laddy would run and jump and play. If Kenny was sad, Laddy would hover close to the boy so he wouldn't feel alone. Laddy was always there for Kenny. He even met Kenny's bus each afternoon to walk him home from school. Laddy protected Kenny and loved him unconditionally.

One day, Laddy and Kenny were chasing each other through the woods. Laddy was winning the race but was quickly distracted when he saw a rabbit dart through the bushes. Kenny stopped to watch as the dog leaped into the air to try and catch the little animal but landed smack-dab into a pine tree instead. Kenny started laughing. A little dazed and confused, Laddy emerged from the tree, covered in pine needles. He also had a pinecone stuck to his ear. Kenny doubled over in laughter. He didn't notice the big hole in the ground, however, and tripped, twisting his leg.

The dog whined and paced the yard the entire time the boy was at the hospital. When Kenny came home with his leg in a cast, Laddy held constant vigil by the boy's bedside. If Kenny needed a book to read, Laddy would run and get it for him. If Kenny needed to scratch his back, Laddy would bring him a stick. If Kenny was thirsty, Laddy would go and find Kenny's mother.

The dog even gave up his daily hole-digging activity while Kenny was bedridden. Laddy didn't even give chase when the cat came around.

The Bible tells us that a true friend should love at all times (see Proverbs 17:17). We should love each other when things are going well, but we should also love during the hard times. God wants us to carry each other's burdens and help out whenever we can. We should be willing to give up our "hole-digging," or our planned activities for the day, when a friend is in need. Good friends laugh when its time to laugh and mourn when its time to mourn. Ask the Lord how you can be a better friend to those He has placed in your life.

jessie and the Potbellied Pigs

DEE ASPIN

*"I no longer call you servants, because a servant does not know his
master's business. Instead, I have called you friends."*
JOHN 15:15 NIV

Friends come in all sizes, shapes, and species. Jessie was a tall, fun-loving, red setter with flowing hair. Her girlfriends, Bridgette and Sassy, lived on the ranch with her. They were short, round potbellied pigs. Every spring when the plum trees bore fruit, the piggies stood on their hind legs, grabbed the plums with their mouths, ripped them from the branches, and knocked them down to the ground to eat. It wasn't too much of a loss until Lorraine, their master, noticed more fruit disappearing higher up on the trees.

Lorraine was puzzled until one serendipitous morning when she discovered the cause and the culprit.

Jessie was standing tall on her hind legs, grabbing the fruit with her mouth and throwing it to the ground with vigorous intent. The piggies grunted, waiting impatiently below to guzzle up the red ripe fruit dropping like candy from a piñata. Jessie would do anything for her girlfriends—even if it meant getting in trouble with Lorraine.

One morning Lorraine was rubbing her piggy's tummies after they both flopped down in front of her—one to the right and one to the left—leaving a space between them. Their tails wriggled in glee. Jessie, who had been observing from a distance, then walked over, faced Lorraine, and lay down in the space between Bridgette and Sassy. She flipped belly-up in front of Lorraine for her tummy rub, too.

Friends are wonderful to share life with. We never know when they will come along or what they will look like. We may share daily routines with them or new activities they teach us to enjoy. They stay with us when we need a helping hand or paw.

We can always recognize our friends—they love us just the way we are. They will tell us if there is food between our teeth, yet not try to change us. They like our character and personality, grateful we are different from them no matter how many unique idiosyncrasies and special mannerisms we have.

True friends accept each other just as Jesus told us: Accept one another as I have accepted you. Be kind to one another and devoted to one another.

God doesn't ask us to do anything less than what He demonstrated for us at the Last Supper. Jesus washed the feet of His disciples. He served them by caring for their physical needs and humbling Himself. Jessie humbled herself and shared the ground with her pig friends. She got right in between them and shared the experience they were having with her master.

Jesus died on a cross between two thieves. He spoke to each while He was dying. One recognized Jesus was a Friend and Savior who really loved him. He asked for forgiveness and Jesus invited him to be with Him that very day in Paradise. Our friends want to be with us and, amazingly, so does our Creator who sent His Son. God is our Master, our Friend.

Cat Butter

DEE ASPIN

Be devoted to one another in brotherly love.
Honor one another above yourselves.

ROMANS 12:10 NIV

Marie had purchased her cat, Pike, at a hardware store. Culled from a box full of fluffy kittens, Pike turned into a gorgeous long-white-haired prince. Ten pounds of kitty willpower and three years later, Marie bought a puppy.

Benny was a half Lab–half pit puppy she picked up at the shelter after he was found in a Dumpster. He grew to a mere ninety pounds seemingly overnight.

However, Marie had a problem. Benny didn't like Pike. For a year and a half, her pets avoided each other like the plague. That is, until one day when she made a mistake.

"One day I ran out of Petromalt, a cat lube to prevent hairballs," Marie explained. "I used butter instead. I put a big glob on my finger and, placing him on his back in my lap, I shoved it down Pike's throat. He didn't want to be force-fed, so he fought me. I lost half of it all over his face. Instead of my lubing his head, he got basted. Then he jumped down, completely disgusted.

"I noticed Benny's nose in the air, sniffing with laser focus, while the cat left me on the floor. When I realized Pike was out of my reach, my heart started racing.

" 'Please don't eat the cat! Please don't eat the cat!' I shouted, powerless to intervene. Then something amazing happened.

"To my utter shock, the cat, prancing around with a condiment on his head, stopped in front of Benny. Benny looked down in rapturous delight. His tongue, as big as Pike's head, proceeded to lick every ounce of butter off Pike's head.

"The cat rolled his neck and head around while Benny licked with all his might. Pike was getting a deep massage—it was sheer delight—until every ounce of butter was gone. And my cat was still there! The butter was consumed, but the cat wasn't."

After this, everything changed. Pike and Benny became fast friends. They still frequently sleep on the bed together.

What happened that day? Benny realized the value of the cat. Pike treated him to the butter without a fuss. In fact, Pike made it easier for him to get all the butter off by moving his head around. Pike appreciated Benny taking off all that goop. Benny could groom Pike in places Pike could never get to. . .and he got a good head massage to boot.

Sometimes, we don't appreciate someone until something happens where we realize we need this person to help us. We really aren't as independent as we think. In fact, if some people weren't around, things might get pretty sticky from time to time, just like Pike discovered.

Unfortunately, the truth is we all take each other for granted. And it usually is more so toward those in our own daily lives—the ones we encounter every day.

But then the car breaks down. . .and who do we call to come pick us up? Maybe we just left the house, snarling about this person minutes before. Who do we call when a sudden emergency arises? Hopefully we will all wake up and smell the butter, just like Pike and Benny.

the tag-team Doorbell

DEE ASPIN

Now you are the body of Christ, and each one of you is a part of it.
1 CORINTHIANS 12:27 NIV

When Aaron and Nancy were missionaries in Mexico, before having their children, they had two Australian shepherds, Buddy and Tara. Tara could see, but she could not hear. She was partially deaf. Buddy could hear, but he could not see. He was partially blind.

Houses in Mexico are made of solid brick, which provide a great sound barrier. Aaron and Nancy's property, typical for their village, had iron gates around it to keep out thieves. This worked great, except when visitors came. Their house was located so far into the property and away from the gate that Aaron and Nancy couldn't even have heard Avon calling.

Buddy and Tara became the answer. As a tag-team doorbell, they worked great together. Buddy's ears would perk up, because he could hear someone was at the front gate but he could not see them. Tara couldn't hear them, but she could see Buddy's ears alarming her like silent radar—prompting her to start working her way around to the front gate.

She would race around to the front, barking all the way. If it was a friend she recognized, she immediately headed down the path to the front door and scratched and barked. Thus alerted by Tara, Nancy and Aaron—who could hardly hear a thing inside their brick fortress—would head out of the house to let their visitor in.

If it was a stranger, Tara would bark and growl and scare the solicitor away. Together, the tag-team let Nancy and Aaron know if they had a visitor or if they were protecting them from a break-in. Together they worked as a doorbell.

Tara and Buddy functioned well together. They were a great unit. Each needed the other to make a first-class doorbell. In the same way they worked for the good of the whole. First Corinthians 12 talks about the church as the body of Christ, which is made of many members. Each member has a part to ensure the entire body functions well as a whole: "A spiritual gift is given to each of us so we can help each other" (1 Corinthians 12:7 NLT). "The eye cannot say to the hand, 'I don't need you!' And the head cannot say to the feet, 'I don't need you!'" (1 Corinthians 12:21 NIV).

In our singles' ministry at church, different people gifted in a variety of ways worked together to build a thriving ministry. The hospitality group could not say to the worship team, "I don't need you." The Bible study teachers could not say to the events team, "I don't need you." The coordinators could not say to childcare workers, "I don't need you." The speaker could not say to the sound tech, "I don't need you."

We function well together when we each do our part and when we live with the understanding God has given us each a place in His body that is valuable.

Happy

RACHEL QUILLIN

A merry heart maketh a cheerful countenance:
but by sorrow of the heart the spirit is broken.
PROVERBS 15:13 KJV

You know that silly grin on most dogs' faces? A good many dogs appear to find life quite entertaining, and why not? They don't have a care in the world. Their meals are served to them in personalized dishes. They have nice warm beds or at least straw-lined doghouses where they spend their time dreaming of chasing cars, tormenting less vicious creatures, or having their bellies rubbed. Ahh, the privileged lives they lead.

Happy the hound, however, is not happy. At least she doesn't appear to be happy. She waddles around with a pathetic look and her face nearly dragging on the ground. Her countenance is evidence that all her efforts are halfhearted at best.

Truthfully there is no way the dog would ever appear to live up to her name. She's a floppy-eared, wrinkly skinned basset hound—proof that God has a sense of humor obvious even in His creation. Every pet lover has preferences as to what type of animal they keep, and I suppose it's good for all the "Happys" out there that someone loves them. They just always look so sad. You might think they carried the weight of the world on their shoulders.

Typically when a person approaches a dog, he can determine pretty quickly how the dog feels about his presence. There's the telltale wag of the tail and excited pant that says the dog was just waiting for someone to welcome. On the other hand, some dogs will greet you with a snarl and a snap of the jaws that lets you know you are quite possibly overstepping your bounds.

If Happy is feeling particularly energetic, she might meander up to you out of mere curiosity rather than any real care about your existence. On lazy days she is more likely to observe from a distance. About the only thing that can truly raise her ire is a cat that crosses too closely in her path. Even at that, her expression never changes.

It's easy to feel sorry for the poor thing. She just doesn't seem to fit in. Of course, she doesn't know this, and neither do the other dogs. They get along just fine. They don't worry about her mopey-looking eyes or the fact that we humans want to attribute emotions that might or might not exist. She is what she is; take it or leave it.

So she's a basset hound, and she's supposed to look like that. People are not. The expression on a person's face often tells very much about her. A person with a happy expression is generally more pleasant to be around than someone with a sour look, because what's on your face reflects what's in your soul.

Did you know that the average child laughs 150 times each day? The average adult is closer to 15. Why is this? Well, in general, adults do have more to be concerned about than children do, but that sounds like more of an excuse than a reason. Perhaps we need to practice laughing more until it becomes second nature. Read a joke book; watch a funny movie; play a crazy game. Watch silly kids—or silly animals. Enjoy the humor God has blessed you with. Your friends—and your face—will thank you.

Louie the Lighthearted Lab

MILLIE McCLOY

Our mouths were filled with laughter, our tongues with songs of joy.
PSALM 126:2 NIV

Louie bounced up the stairs, shoved the bedroom door open, and leaped onto the bed. The boys awoke with a start and squealed with delight as Louie grabbed the covers in his mouth and pulled them to the floor. Both boys jumped from bed and chased Louie around the room a few times before Louie ran to the bathroom and jumped into the shower. Michael and Matthew knew this was Louie's way of getting them up and ready.

No two days were exactly the same. Louie was a fun-loving pup. He was always spontaneous and animated. He was truly God's gift to the twins.

After the boys brushed their teeth and dressed, Louie bounded down the stairs and slid across the kitchen floor toward his empty bowls. He picked up his food bowl and met the boys' mother just as she was placing the box of cereal and milk on the table. Mrs. Brunch let out a laugh as Louie gently nudged her to hurry.

Louie usually finished his meal first and then would wander to the table and gently lay his muzzle on the table—wide eyed and drooling—as if to tell the boys he was done.

Breakfast behind them, the twins washed their hands, and raced to the backyard. This was Louie's playground!

Louie climbed the steps of the slide and plunged headfirst toward the ground, landing with a face plant, grass in his teeth. Matthew and Michael tackled Louie before he could get up, and they rolled around giggling.

Louie leaped around in a circle, squatted on his front paws, and barked loudly to egg them on. The boys grabbed a football and started to toss it back and forth. Louie leaped into the air, faked a catch, then circled around as though running yardage.

When the boys went swimming that afternoon, Louie cannon-balled into the water with such force the entire patio got a shower, including Mr. and Mrs. Brunch. Louie lunged underwater to tease the boys and retrieve a few lost water toys.

That night as Mom and Dad knelt beside Matthew and Michael for night prayers, Louie, too, placed his front paws on the bed and bowed his head. As needs were made known and blessings acknowledged, the boys thanked God, yet again, for their gentle, loving, fun-filled friend, Louie.

PUPPY DOG EYES: KEEPING FOCUSED ON THE HEAVENLY FATHER

When a dog eagerly wags his tail, all his attention
is focused on the person in his line of vision.
Has God enjoyed such focused attention from [you] today?
KATHERINE DOUGLAS

Small Trips and Special Places

DEE ASPIN

But godliness with contentment is great gain. For we brought nothing into the world and we can take nothing out of it.

1 TIMOTHY 6:6–7 NIV

So how was your outing?" our friend Gary asked from somewhere under the truck as Sam, Benji, and I stepped into the garage from our dog walk. His monster Tonka rested wheel-less on small metal stands. Tools littered the garage floor like clothes in a teenager's room as he peeked at us from under the greasy engine, wearing a grimy torn shirt.

"It's beautiful," I crooned. "The stars are shining brightly, and it's a cool summer night." The hands of my watch ticked past eleven o'clock.

Gary's hands reached to pat a big pink nose and stroke a small fluffy ear.

"Sammy especially enjoyed it." I grinned at the shining eyes of my yellow Lab and recounted his casual glances toward the direction of neighboring nocturnal canines. They'd barked jealously from behind the confines of six-foot wooden planks, boards that separated them from the rest of the world of adventure—our side of the fence.

"Sammy cocked his head and smiled toward his exasperated peers as if to say, 'I'm having the time of my life—too bad you're stuck back there.'"

"Well, he's been doing the same thing all day!" Gary's voice rose. "He and Benji have been barking at everyone who passed by today."

Sometimes, I get restless, too. I become restless wishing I were going on an adventure when neighbors drive by toward the lake with their boats hitched to the back of their trucks, or mountain bikes hanging on their SUV racks. But then, just pulling out the leashes for a walk with Benji and Sammy and feeling *their* excitement for a small jaunt around our neighborhood, gives me a sense of peace and calm pleasure.

No matter how many times they've been by that bush on the corner, they are delighted to sniff it again. Or the beloved fire hydrants on our route. It's enough. By the time they get home, they sprawl out, content for the rest of the day. They don't really need a big trip to the river—anywhere beyond our territory will do.

A simple daily walk makes all the difference in their mental and emotional state. They dogtrot to the joggers and walkers, confident they are connected to the bigger picture beyond the window pane. As other dogs saunter by us on the sidewalk, my dogs smile at me and carry themselves proudly, as if our expedition beats any Lassie episode paws down.

It helps me realize I minimize the easy, simple, and free adventures God offers me daily. Grateful just to use my legs and appreciate the value of small steps into ordinary places, familiar faces, and friendly hellos. The territory God has given us is our neighborhood. If these small walks are enough to make Sammy smile at me and put a spring in Benji's steps, then it is enough to evoke an energetic response of gratitude from me to my Creator.

Assume the Position

JANICE HANNA

Then Jesus told his disciples a parable to show them that they should always pray and not give up. He said: "In a certain town there was a judge who neither feared God nor cared about men. And there was a widow in that town who kept coming to him with the plea, 'Grant me justice against my adversary.' For some time he refused. But finally he said to himself, 'Even though I don't fear God or care about men, yet because this widow keeps bothering me, I will see that she gets justice, so that she won't eventually wear me out with her coming!'"
LUKE 18:1–5 NIV

Riley was a long, lean dachshund. He was also extremely patient and determined. From the time he was a little pup, he figured out how to get his master's attention: He would assume the begging position. Riley had this down to a science. Up he would go on his haunches, his back perfectly straight, his head at a ninety-degree angle and his front paws in a lovely begging posture. All the while his gaze remained fixed on his master. There he would remain until she finally looked his way and gave him what he wanted.

Sometimes Riley would sit in this position for fifteen or twenty minutes until he happened to catch his master's eye. The determined pup didn't mind the wait because he knew it would pay off in the end. When he wanted scraps from the table, he would assume the position. When he wanted up on the bed, his prayerful pose would win over his master in a heartbeat. When he wanted his tummy tickled or his ears scratched, he knew just what to do. Assume the position.

Peggy, his master, would always get tickled when she found Riley begging, in part because of his persistence. And she marveled at how long he would go on in that posture, his back as straight as an arrow. Surely the little guy must get tired of holding himself perfectly still, right? There was something to be said for his tenacity.

As believers, we need to take our cues from Riley. The Bible says that we are to pray without ceasing. When times are tough, we need to "assume the position" in prayer and hold steady, even when circumstances around us aren't changing. We need to keep on giving thanks, particularly when we don't feel like it. And our petitions to the Father should be ongoing, even when we feel like we're not getting answers.

Consider the story of the widow woman and the judge. Her persistence finally won the judge over, in much the same way Riley eventually won his master over. There's something about a person who just won't give up that touches the heart of a loving master. And it does us good to persevere in prayer, for in doing so our faith is increased.

Today, take inventory. Have you given up on something? Stopped asking? Assume the position. . .in prayer. Make your petitions known to the Lord. Approach His throne boldly, with confidence, and know that your heavenly Father's heart is touched by your tenacity.

A Fluttering of Wings

DONNA K. MALTESE

"Whoever believes in me, as the Scripture has said,
streams of living water will flow from within him."
JOHN 7:38 NIV

The severe drought our area of Pennsylvania suffered during the summer of 1999 took its toll on the lives of the old and weak, which included our eleven-year-old German shepherd mutt Buckingham. Less than two weeks after his departure, we brought life back into our quiet and seemingly empty house with a new pound puppy, a German shepherd-border collie mix we named Schaefer. And with the puppy, came, amazingly enough, the rains that replenished our wells and overflowed our creeks.

In his new backyard, Schaefer ate the ripe mulberries that dropped into our driveway, and teethed on porch pillars and tree trunks. Every time we threw him a ball, he'd run away from it.

Days after his arrival, Schaefer and I took a walk into the woods. When he saw the creek, he ran up to the water's edge, then turned back, running in circles on the pebbled shore. Then he'd dash down to the water again, each time going in deeper, although never past his belly fur.

Schaefer chased leaves on the shore and sticks in the stream. Water bugs hopped right in front of his nose but he never seemed to see them. Then, exhausted, the puppy lay down among the weeds and new green patches of grass. Later, on our way back down the forest path, Schaefer spotted a fluttering of wings. He started to chase the butterfly. But whenever it flew out of his vision, the puppy assumed it had flown off the face of the earth. Yet from my vantage point, I could see that if he would just turn his head or look up, he would find what he was seeking. But soon, the puppy was back sniffing the ground, rolling in the weeds, tripping over his own paws, and licking up ants.

Sometimes what we seek is fluttering around our heads, shoulders, arms, legs, and we are simply not seeing it. We are too easily distracted, too quickly resigned, too lazy to reach out, too tired to hope. But no matter what we are lacking or what is outside our perception, if we persist in our hopes, continue with our prayers, keep our faith in God, and pursue our visions, only then will we find what we so desperately seek.

We wait. We pray for what we once took for granted. We wait. We pray for God's hand upon us. We wait. We pray for our creeks to run swiftly, for our wells to be replenished, for our throats to be wet, for a new puppy to heal the loss of the old dog we loved so much.

Keep your faith and hope alive. Turn your head toward the fluttering of wings. Set your sights beyond the cloudless sky, bathe the world in prayer, and you will replenish the earth and your soul with living water as you capture the once elusive butterfly of your dreams.

tea for two

JANICE HANNA

Satan will not outsmart us. For we are familiar with his evil schemes.
2 CORINTHIANS 2:11 NLT

Nancy was a single woman in her sixties who loved spending time curled up in her recliner by the fireplace with a great book. Sitting next to her on the end table. . .a cup of chai latte, her beverage of choice. Buffy, Nancy's aging Yorkshire terrier, loved these quiet evenings by the fire next to her owner. The two were a perfect match.

One evening after a long stretch of reading, Nancy got up from her recliner to fetch a couple of cookies from the kitchen. She left her cooled cup of chai latte on the end table, not thinking a thing about it. When she returned with the cookies, Nancy was stunned to find the cup empty. She racked her brain, trying to remember. . . . "Did I drink all of that tea?" Thinking perhaps she had, she took the cup back to the kitchen to rinse it out. Afterward, she returned to find the cookies gone, too!

Nancy looked down at the little Yorkie, who looked up with crumbs all over her face. The little thief soon began to race around the room, energized by the caffeine and sugar. Yep. Looked like Buffy had stolen the goods! What a sneak!

From that day on, the wary owner kept a watchful eye on her food products and beverages, especially the chai latte, which Buffy seemed to love. She figured out the dog's well thought-out scheme...to steal when Nancy's back was turned. No more. Buffy didn't need the caffeine, and Nancy didn't need to be outwitted by a five-pound dog.

Do you ever feel like Nancy? Feel like someone is sneaking around behind your back, trying to steal from you? If so, you're not alone. Oftentimes we leave ourselves open to the enemy's schemes by letting our guard down. Looking the other way. Leaving the room. We make ourselves vulnerable, but don't even know it.

When we're distracted, the enemy puts his nose in where it doesn't belong. He robs us. What does he reach for first? Our joy, of course. Then he snags our peace. Next he messes with our finances. When we're completely vulnerable, he reaches for our relationships. Unfortunately, we're often so beaten down or frazzled at this point that we fold like a deck of cards. We give up, unwilling to fight back. And all because we weren't paying attention in the first place.

Sound familiar? Maybe you're going through a season where you've become vulnerable to the enemy's attacks. If so, you need to recognize his schemes. He's got a specific plan of action and it's based on your weaknesses. He knows you well, after all, and doesn't mind striking below the belt. Today, take the time to ask the Lord to show you when and how the enemy is attempting to steal from you. God will give you the wisdom you need to claim victory over even the sneakiest of schemes.

Watching and Waiting

MariLee Parrish

*"You also must be ready all the time, for the
Son of Man will come when least expected."*
Luke 12:40 nlt

Bud and Alex were alone while their masters were at work each day, but they didn't mind one bit. The two golden retrievers spent the day exploring their backyard, playing with chew toys, and chasing each other around the house. Although the dogs usually kept their mischief to a minimum, some days a new discovery was worth the risk of getting into trouble when their owners came home . . .like when the dogs discovered the Crock-Pot.

The dogs had smelled something yummy right from the start. They saw the appliance on the counter and knew that the delicious smell was coming from that pot. For most of the day the dogs tried to ignore the meaty aroma. They chased a rabbit in the backyard, played a few games of hide-and-seek, and tried hard to forget what could only be considered as the best thing they had ever smelled in their entire lives. But as the day grew on, the smell kept getting stronger and more delicious. By late afternoon, the dogs could not resist any longer. Sinking their chops into whatever was hiding in the large pot was definitely worth whatever punishment might come.

Bud climbed up on the counter and took a hold of the lid with his teeth. He pulled it off the pot and dropped it on the counter. Alex climbed up after him and both dogs started in on the giant, melt-in-your-mouth roast. Knowing that their masters would be home any minute, the dogs took turns eating. One dog would stand at the edge of the kitchen, watching and listening for the garage door, while the other one would help himself to the feast. Then they would switch.

The dogs had been eating and watching for only a few minutes when they heard the garage door go up. Intelligent as he was, Bud tried to get the lid back on the Crock-Pot but was unsuccessful. Alex was barking, warning Bud to run and hide, but his masters walked into the kitchen and caught him red-handed. Or rather red-jawed.

The Bible tells us that Jesus could come back anytime, when we least expect it. Instead of Christ returning to find you doing something you shouldn't be doing, be ready for Him. Live your life in such a way that if Jesus came back today, He would be pleased with what you are doing and how you are living. We do not know the day or the hour, but be assured that He will return. He has gone to prepare a place for us in heaven and has promised to come back and take us along with Him. Will you be ready?

Unlikely Leader

RACHEL QUILLIN

These be the names of the mighty men whom
David had. . .thirty and seven in all.
2 SAMUEL 23:8, 39 KJV

Living on a farm among the rolling hills of southeastern Ohio has provided us with countless opportunities to enjoy the comic relief that God's creation provides. It is a family farm, and by that I mean four households are part of the setting. At any given time each household includes at least one dog. Currently there are six resident dogs, but that is, of course, subject to change at a moment's notice.

Each dog is different in kind, size, shape, and personality. One among them is the born leader—a Yorkshire terrier named Scruffy. The rest of the dogs, with the exception of the grouchy old Red Heeler who keeps to herself, follow Scruffy around as if he were the head honcho, which he, of course, believes that he is.

The thing of it is that Scruffy is small. He's the smallest dog of the pack, and Molly is his most loyal subject. Molly is not small. She is a Saint Bernard. Spicy, too, follows him faithfully. She's a big dog, too, but she may well be feeling her age, which would explain her willingness to turn the leadership over to the young blood. Happy the hound is definitely a follower. When the rest of the dogs howl, Happy howls. When they chase cats, she chases cats. When they run down the middle of the road she does her best to keep up. Whatever "they" do, she does, and "they" do whatever Scruffy does. Finally there's Misty, the baby of the bunch, and the sweetest little English shepherd you ever did see. Only she's not so little either. Yet she's content to let Scruffy take charge.

It really is a ridiculous sight to see this group of canine companions running around with this tiny little should-be lap dog leading the way. So why do the big gals follow the little guy? He's established himself in the leadership position. So far he hasn't let them down (although he's come mighty close on more than one occasion where the road is involved). Scruffy's good at what he does (i.e., chasing cats and protecting the premises from prowlers, be they human or otherwise). He has not allowed his youth or his lack of size to keep him from doing what dogs consider great things.

Although Scruffy often annoys me, I have to admit he's a lot like David. Remember, he was the youngest of Jesse's sons, and he was so small he couldn't stand up in King Saul's armor. That didn't intimidate him though. He pressed on, acquired a band of loyal followers, and aside from Jesus Christ, became Israel's greatest king.

Was David perfect? Of course not. Is Scruffy perfect? Absolutely not! Perfection is not what makes a great leader. Faithfulness and obedience to God are the first steps in the right direction. You can make a difference in your community by choosing to take a stand to live a godly life. You might think there are those who are better equipped or stronger in their faith. Give your fears to God and let Him turn them into qualities that will make you a great spiritual leader with a following comprised of people who will also someday be great leaders themselves.

the Dogs of Christmas Day

KATHERINE DOUGLAS

And when they were come into the house, they saw the young child with
Mary his mother, and fell down, and worshipped him: and when they
had opened their treasures, they presented unto him gifts; gold,
and frankincense and myrrh.

MATTHEW 2:11 KJV

Lifelong human friends, Margaret and Juanita, began their early morning walk Christmas Day. As they started out, three large dogs came bounding up the street, obviously enjoying their Christmas romp in the dawning Florida sun. Each member of the threesome, black as polished ebony, sniffed about for food. Their collars had no identifying numbers, computer chips, or names. They belonged to someone, but whom? Margaret and Juanita called their neighbors, volunteers with the Society for the Prevention of Cruelty to Animals.

"Bring them on over," their friends said. "We'll try to locate their owners."

Enticing the dogs with treats, the finders lured the hungry trio to the garage of the SPCA volunteers. When the three dogs saw the goodies set out for them, they eagerly devoured their Christmas breakfast.

No one ever claimed or came for the threesome. After special care by the SPCA, the dogs were made avaiLable for adoption. A family adopted the trio on New Year's Day, and kept them together.

Because Margaret and Juanita found the dogs wandering in their particular neighborhood, they decided they were wise dogs. Here it was, Christmas Day. The dogs chose a street where kind people took an interest in them. They went into a place where they were fed and kept safe. They submitted to their caretakers until a good home could be found. These wise dogs showed up at the right time, on the right day, on the right street. Maggie and Juanita named these three dogs of Christmas appropriately: Gold, Frankincense, and Myrrh—the names they've kept to this day!

The shepherds, the only ones on record who saw the newborn King at His birth on that first Christmas, brought no gifts. They were too eager to get to Bethlehem "and see this thing that has happened, which the Lord has told us about" (Luke 2:15 NIV). Only after a passage of time (most scholars estimate it was about two years) did anyone come with gifts. After searching and making inquiry, these Magi ("wise men" in the King James version of Matthew 2:1) came to Bethlehem. With the God-given leading of a special star, they found the house where "the young child" (Matthew 2:9 KJV) and His human parents lived.

It wasn't to the adults that the wise men offered their lavish gifts, but to the child Himself. "And when they were come into the house, they saw the young child. . .and fell down, and worshipped him: and when they had opened their treasures, they presented unto him gifts" (Matthew 2:11 KJV)—the first gifts of Christmas. Before the Magi gave the Christ their gifts, they gave Him their worship.

What will you do with your next Christmas? Will you, like those wise dogs, Gold, Frankincense, and Myrrh, run to the One who alone can meet all your needs? Once you've eagerly sought Him out, will you, too, bow before Him? Then, before offering the King of kings anything you may have, will you, like the Magi of old, first worship Him?

Hearing vs. Heeding and the Oil Spill

SHELLEY LEE

He who enters by the door is the shepherd of the sheep. The watchman opens the door for this man, and the sheep listen to his voice and heed it; and he calls his own sheep by name and brings (leads) them out. When he has brought his own sheep outside, he walks on before them, and the sheep follow him because they know his voice.

JOHN 10:2–4 AMP

I'd been running full tilt all day at work and was now heading home. In the news since early morning was an oil spill that originated on the river one mile south of my house. The report of a few hundred gallons spilled over to several thousand gallons, bringing national news attention and a 24/7 disaster crew stationed at the bridge at the corner of our property. No matter. It was unfortunate, but life would have to clip along for my family.

Relieved to be so near home I rolled over the river bridge past the clean-up posse and its fleet on both sides of the road with massive scattered mud chunks. Attempting to reach my mailbox as I neared the home stretch, where a Crock-Pot of hot stew and a couch (in my dreams) awaited, I noted a herculean Tonka truck blocking my way. So I pulled over into my yard in the cold winter wind to retrieve the day's deliveries. What was a little mud on my dress boots and a few stares from guys wearing geek gear anyway? (They were wearing *huge* safety goggles!)

Back on course as I drove up the country drive, finger on the garage door remote, I noticed a little mud smudge on my nice black overcoat. I quickly forgot about it when I noticed that the dog did not greet me in the yard. Maybe my husband had come home earlier and left her in the house, I thought.

Nope, not in the house. Plans all out of kilter now, I went into hyper-search mode, dropped my work bag inside, and got back into the car to peruse the neighborhood, calling for Zoey. She wasn't next door, nor at the farm across the street. *Please God, not across the river and all the way down that long lane.*

Retracing my tracks, I pass the goggle guys for more stares. Bouncing down the country lane I saw the river lined with goggle guys, one of whom told me there was a dog down in the river with the boat crew.

In the river? Boat crew? By the time I arrived back home and ran across my yard, my fingers were nearly as frigid as my attitude. Standing at the top of the riverbank in my muddy boots, I spotted Zoey at the water's edge, covered in oil, and buddying it up boat side with the goggle guys.

When I called her she stood like a stone with eyes, then after some thought decided to work her way up the bank. When she got close she looked at me as if I were an alien, and ran in the other direction. The chase escalated to a fevered pitch of running, grabbing, and wrestling her back. Oil, mud, and all, we made it home where a lot of laundering and a serious dog bath got me thinking.

How many times has God come for me when I've strayed and I didn't really want to see Him? How many times did He love me anyway and clean me up, even when I didn't heed His call? And in the end His love won out. And that's all that matters.

How Many Lives Do Dogs Have?

RACHEL QUILLIN

Jesus said unto her, I am the resurrection, and the life: he that believeth in me, though he were dead, yet shall he live.

JOHN 11:25 KJV

It is said that cat's have nine lives. As far as I know, the same has not been said for dogs. One particular Jack Russell, aptly named Russ (because *all* male Jack Russells on our farm are named Russ—and yes, most of the females are Jackie) seemed to forget for a day that he was, in fact, not feline. Of all the beautiful acres to explore, it appears that those nearest the road are the most attractive. While our farm is lovely, it is not along one of those idyllic little country roads or dirt lanes but smack dab on the curve of a rather highly, and quickly, traveled road. It is probably not the best playground for small dogs, but they obviously forget the near-misses and return for the thrill of adventure or whatever it is that attracts them to such perils.

So on that otherwise beautiful morning, Russ was taking a stroll along the road when around the curve and at a high rate of speed came a car and its mad driver. It took Russ so much by surprise that he had no opportunity to react. Before he knew what was happening, he was lying on the side of the road, still breathing, hanging on to threads of life but all too close to becoming another statistic of involuntary canine-slaughter.

In those same seconds, the car came to a screeching halt, and its badly shaken driver was at Russ's side, willing the little creature to be alive. Soon my husband arrived on the scene. The driver tearfully begged him to allow her to try to nurse Russ back to health. Seeing the hopelessness of the situation, he kindly declined the offer and made Russ as comfortable as possible in the barn. He checked on the little dog from time to time, and Russ continued to pathetically hang on. A few hours later he was gone. Literally. He had disappeared. We figured he had dragged himself off somewhere to die alone, not even giving us a chance to give him a proper burial.

Of course, it wouldn't have been very nice of us to bury him alive, and that was very much the case. He wasn't slowly making his way around or playing the invalid of earlier in the day. Apparently he couldn't stand much of that because the next time we saw him, which was hours after the mishap, he was running around, happy as you please, just like nothing had happened.

That's what happens when a person trusts Christ as Savior. Prior to salvation, we are dead in our sin. We are living a pitiful existence with no hope at all. That's why Christ died and rose again, though. He defeated sin and when we trust Him as Savior, He robs the grave of another victim (see 1 Corinthians 15:55–57). What a wonderful promise of new life. Unlike cats, and maybe Russ, we don't get nine lives. It's important that we give the one we do have to Jesus so that we might have eternal life.

DOG DAYS:
OVERCOMING TRIALS

*There is no psychiatrist in the world like a
puppy licking your face.*
BERNARD WILLIAMS

Hurricane Schaefer

DONNA K. MALTESE

He reached down from on high and took hold of me; he drew me out of deep waters. . . . He makes my feet like the feet of a deer; he enables me to stand on the heights. . . . Exalted be God my Savior!

PSALM 18:16, 33, 46 NIV

On September 17, 1999, the morning after Hurricane Floyd hit our area of Pennsylvania, my husband pulled me out of dreamland by throwing our puppy Schaefer, a black and tan German-shepherd–border-collie mix, into our bedroom before he left for work. I tried to ignore the intrusion by shoving my head beneath my pillow, but to no avail. First I had to spring out of bed to rescue leather moccasins from puppy jaws of death. Then to retrieve a tissue from his shredder teeth, a potted hibiscus from his shoveling snout, and a blue towel from his wringer grip. Finally, realizing a "puppy watch" was in effect and that I needed to be awake and alert, I decided to begin my morning devotions. But first I had to run to the bathroom and then grab my Bible from downstairs.

I quickly donned my denim jumper to ward off the morning chill, then momentarily shut the bedroom door on Schaefer. I could hear the puppy whining and scratching at the door as I ran around the house.

Moments later, I shot back up the steps, reached for the knob, turned, and *slam*—my body hit the immovable bedroom door. I turned the knob again. Nothing. It was locked. In his frenzy to get out of the bedroom, the puppy had pushed down the side lever of the old lock box. The destructive force of Hurricane Schaefer was inside my bedroom. And I was locked outside in the hallway.

All the commotion had driven my then nine-year-old son Zach out of bed. While he yawned and scratched his head, I filled him in on the details of my dilemma.

"There's only one thing I can do," I said. "Crawl out the bathroom window, cross the roof, and go in through the bedroom window. Um . . .you do remember the emergency number, right?"

"9-1-1?"

"Right! Stand by." I swallowed back my acrophobia, thanked God for the clothes I'd thrown on my back before leaving my bedroom, and prayed I hadn't locked that particular bedroom window against the rage of yesterday's Hurricane Floyd. Sweeping toilet paper rolls, puzzle books, and pens off the bathroom window sill, I carefully opened the window and screen, pulled myself onto the sill, and then launched one bare foot through the opening. I began crawling across the roof, sweat pouring from my brow. Finally, I reached the window, gripped the outside frame, and grabbed the window sash. It opened!

"Thank God!"

I cleared the sill of a plastic Godzilla and spider plant, then jumped down onto the bedroom carpet. The puppy stood there looking at me, a mixture of shock and relief upon his whiskered muzzle. I'd made it!

I looked at our digital alarm clock. It was only 6:17 a.m., and I'd already survived two hurricanes—Floyd and Schaefer. I pray you will survive whatever hurricanes life brings your way—and praise God in the process.

Bush Whacked

DEE ASPIN

Be still, and know that I am God.
PSALM 46:10 KJV

Today everything started as usual upon entering our place where the Big Yellow Lab and the Little Silver Schnauzer run free—an enclosed church parking lot. Big Sam barked relentlessly while I impatiently snapped commands over my right shoulder to the backseat barker. "Quit barking in my ear!" He ignored me. Little Benji skipped all over the front seat, pushing his nose out the crack of the window just to get an early whiff of his favorite range.

As soon as the door opened, Benji shot out like a rock in a slingshot, disappearing from view. Sam's barks continued crescendoing until I flipped a ball from the Chuckit ball launcher, and he lunged after the little round object of his obsession.

I flung the ragged tennis ball with an occasional side-glance to locate Benji. When it was time to leave, Sam climbed in the backseat as usual, panting and guarding his ball in the folds of his blanket.

Benji, who never sits still but weaves in and out of the bushes and smells everything, didn't come. I called and called until I noticed him frowning. He was sitting in the center of a patch of high groundcover and refused to budge. No matter how forceful my tone, he just sat and stared.

Finally I walked over and stood above him. He looked straight up at me. Obviously something was uncomfortable, so I reached down and plucked him straight up from the brush he was sitting in carefully, like lifting up a measuring cup full of oil. As soon as we arrived at the car he hopped in and resumed his usual passenger position.

What was up? I didn't know. I could only guess he felt uncomfortable trying to move in that groundcover. Maybe he was protecting his tender parts. All I know is his behavior had changed quite suddenly.

Sometimes people around us are suddenly quiet or suddenly loud. What is going on? Maybe we need to take a minute and head over in their direction to check the situation out. If Sam needed me he would cry. Not Benji. He holds it in.

God hears our silent cries. He loves us all, even the least, like the lost sheep, the stuck sheep, or sinner. He picks us up like a shepherd and carries us to safety.

Benji didn't show anxiety because he wasn't afraid, knowing I would never leave without him. He is accustomed to me helping him, even picking foxtails from his feet and burs from every wiry hair, after he shuffles through a dry field. He knows I have taken care of him before. Why would I stop today?

Why can't I show the same quiet trust toward the Lord when I get bushwhacked by life? When was the last time I waited, knowing He would make a way for me to escape unharmed from a sticky situation?

Maybe I need to practice active listening if others are suddenly quiet. What is going on if their behavior has changed? All they might need from me is a little boost to get them on their way—just like God helps us.

the Sheepdog and the Shepherd

DEE ASPIN

"I am the good shepherd; I know my sheep and my sheep know me."
JOHN 10:14 NIV

Aaron and Nancy were living in Sacramento and, like many newlyweds, had been thinking of starting their family with a dog. One day they stepped into a pet store, captured by the tiny barks of Australian shepherd puppies. One little female pushed through her fluffy siblings, straight to Nancy and Aaron's feet, and into their hearts—and so their family began.

Over the next few years they wondered if Tara really was a sheepdog or if the storeowners had just said that to sell her. They imagined that, through generations of domestic breeding, she had lost her herding instincts.

That was, until Aaron and Nancy moved to Mexico years later. After attempting to have children of their own, God provided a way for them to adopt two children from an orphanage. Manuel, the boy, was three and Karina, the girl, was two years old when they carried them into their new home.

Now with two toddlers exploring the world, much to Aaron and

Nancy's surprise, Tara's sheepherding instincts immediately kicked in. She saw Manuel and Karina as her sheep—the sheep she never had.

Aaron and Nancy became shepherds. If they were in the house and the children were outside in the yard, all they had to say was, "Time to go." And Tara, their sheepdog, stepped quickly into motion.

"Tara, go get Manuel and Karina!" sent her out the door, beginning to herd her charges. As Manuel and Karina were playing Tara patiently walked toward them sideways and wrapped her body around Karina, the two-year-old, pushing her into the house. Then she would return to Manuel, the three-year-old, and she would scoot him into the house.

When they were down at the beach she stayed with her little flock. If Manuel and Karina wandered too far down the shore for her comfort she would herd them back to Nancy and Aaron. If they toddled too far into the ocean water she'd herd them and bring them back to the sand.

"We didn't need to do anything," Aaron said. "Tara would care for Manuel and Karina, shepherd them and pasture them as if they were her flock, without us saying anything—Tara cared for them."

Jesus is our Shepherd who leads us, guides us, and cares for our needs. He watches us and rounds us up when we are wandering too far away, too long. If we are floundering in deep darkness, He wants to guide us out and get us where we need to be. As a good shepherd, Jesus always cares for His sheep and watches our every step.

Tara didn't round up other children at the beach. She only herded Manuel and Karina. The children responded to Tara and she guided them. Jesus said He knows His sheep. His sheep listen for His voice because they know it. So we learn to recognize the voice of our Shepherd and to trust Him enough to follow Him wherever He leads. It will always be to safety—He always leads us home.

Beyond All We Can Ask or Imagine

DONNA K. MALTESE

Now to him who is able to do immeasurably more than all we ask or imagine, according to his power that is at work within us, to him be glory.

EPHESIANS 3:20–21 NIV

Our dog Schaefer, an SPCA hound, had an abnormal fear of rain (along with thunder, lightning, fireworks, and some people), so when he knew a storm (or any type of rainfall) was coming, he'd start to pant heavily, shake, turn his water bowl over, ravage rolls of toilet paper, and then cower in the shower.

One summer, a friend agreed to watch our house and our half-shepherd, half-border collie hound while we vacationed at the Jersey Shore. Between storms and Fourth of July fireworks, she stopped by to check on our neurotic mongrel. One afternoon, upon entering the house, our friend noticed Schaefer's overturned stainless-steel bowl. There was water all over the kitchen floor and shreds of toilet paper strewn from the kitchen to the powder room. After cleaning up this mess and putting out fresh water, she checked out the upstairs bathroom only to find a shaken Schaefer cowering in the shower stall and the entire bathroom rug crammed into the toilet bowl. As my husband Pete later said, "And to think he did all that without opposable thumbs. Thank God he didn't flush."

Several years later, my family and I went through our own storm when we had to put Schaefer down. We were heartbroken but knew it was for the best. So, after we blew our noses and dried our tears, we went looking for a new dog to love and cherish.

A week later, we brought home a six-month-old puppy from the SPCA and named him Ziggy. Within days, we realized our puppy was lame and dangerously aggressive toward anyone other than our immediate family. Weeks later, our vet diagnosed Ziggy as having severe hip dysplasia. His only possible chance at a normal life was hip replacement, a surgical procedure we could ill afford, and its chances of success almost nil. On the Monday after Thanksgiving, our vet put Ziggy down.

Wounded but not defeated, we went looking for another puppy. Coming down to breakfast one morning, I noticed Pete had left me the phone numbers for two different dog-rescue organizations. I called both, and when my son Zach came home from school, we headed to Durham Road in Rieglesville to check out the last puppy avaiLable at Dogs for Adoption.

As Zach and I walked up the driveway, a wrinkly-headed, yellow-haired puppy came lopping along on the heels of one of the workers. He had the head of a shar-pei and the body of a yellow Lab. As soon as he saw Zach, the pup ran over, knocked him down, and began licking his face. It was love at first sight. That afternoon we brought home a healthy, loving, funny-looking puppy that gnaws on furniture, steals remote controls, digs up and eats dried worms, and has more strength and energy than Superman. We named him

Durham, and he's more than we could have ever asked or imagined.

When circumstances appear to be tearing you apart, shredding your hope, and stomping your dreams, have faith. Look not behind but—with your hand in God's—look forward. For what He will do beyond all you can ask or imagine.

Contributing Authors

Dee Aspin, author, speaker, and life coach, has spent twenty-five years in Christian ministry, currently the Juvenile Justice Chaplaincy. She loves romping with her happy dogs, a yellow Lab, Sammy, and her miniature schnauzer, Benji. A guest writer for CBN.com, she just published her first book *Lord of the Ringless*.

Katherine Douglas's favorite authors are C. S. Lewis and Jan Karon. Her favorite foods are sweet, salty, or chocolate. She loves in-line skating, Bible studies, writing, and encouraging other writers. Kathy has authored several books and dozens of articles. She and her husband make their home in northwest Ohio.

Shelley Lee is a freelance writer who has authored two books and numerous articles. She grew up in Michigan where she met her husband, Dave, at Grand Valley State University. They reside in northwest Ohio with their four sons, a cat, and one dog who loves them all unconditionally.

Donna K. Maltese is the author of Barbour's *Power Prayers to Start Your Day*, a contributor to numerous devotionals, and a creator of puzzles. A freelance writer and editor, she lives in Bucks County, Pennsylvania, is married, and the mother of two grown children.

Chuck Miller lives in Toledo, Ohio. He taught at Toledo Christian High School, has been a hospital chaplain, and currently works as a surgical tech and freelance writer. He has been published in *Dogma* by Katherine Douglas, in *Northcoast* magazine, and in the *Ancient Paths* annual literary anthology, edited by Skylar Burris.

MariLee Parrish lives in Colorado with her husband, Eric, and young son, Jake. She's a freelance musician and writer who desires to paint a picture of God with her life, talents, and ministry.

Rachel Quillin lives with her husband, Eric, and their six children on a dairy farm in Ohio. Her main focus is to serve the Lord in any way possible. She is active in her church, enjoys homeschooling her kids, doing freelance writing when possible, and is never bored!

Paula Swan lives in Toledo, Ohio, with her husband Craig, their rat terriers Jot and Tilly, and their current foster rattie, Kloey. Paula has lived in South America, Canada, and the Republic of South Africa, serving in full-time mission work. She has an AA in World Languages and a BA in Children's Book Development.

Scripture Index

OLD TESTAMENT

NEW TESTAMENT

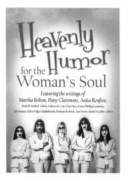